Knowing and Doing: Learning Through Experience

Pat Hutchings, *Editor*
Alverno College

Allen Wutzdorff, *Editor*
Alverno College

NEW DIRECTIONS FOR TEACHING AND LEARNING
ROBERT E. YOUNG, *Editor-in-Chief*
University of Wisconsin

KENNETH E. EBLE, *Consulting Editor*
University of Utah, Salt Lake City

Number 35, Fall 1988

Paperback sourcebooks in
The Jossey-Bass Higher Education Series

Jossey-Bass Inc., Publishers
San Francisco • London

Pat Hutchings, Allen Wutzdorff (eds.).
Knowing and Doing: Learning Through Experience.
New Directions for Teaching and Learning, no. 35.
San Francisco: Jossey-Bass, 1988.

New Directions for Teaching and Learning
Robert E. Young, *Editor-in-Chief*
Kenneth E. Eble, *Consulting Editor*

New Directions for Teaching and Learning is published quarterly
by Jossey-Bass Inc., Publishers, 350 Sansome Street, San Francisco,
California, 94104. Second-class postage paid at San Francisco,
California, and at additional mailing offices. POSTMASTER: Send
address changes to *New Directions for Teaching and Learning,*
Jossey-Bass Inc., Publishers, 350 Sansome Street, San Francisco,
California 94104.

Editorial correspondence should be sent to the Editor-in-Chief,
Robert E. Young, Dean, University of Wisconsin Center, Fox Valley,
1478 Midway Rd., Menasha, Wisconsin 54952.

Library of Congress Catalog Card Number LC 85-644763

International Standard Serial Number ISSN 0271-0633

International Standard Book Number ISBN 1-55542-898-3

Cover art by WILLI BAUM

Manufactured in the United States of America. Printed on acid-free paper.

Ordering Information

The paperback sourcebooks listed below are published quarterly and can be ordered either by subscription or single copy.

Subscriptions cost $52.00 per year for institutions, agencies, and libraries. Individuals can subscribe at the special rate of $39.00 per year *if payment is by personal check*. (Note that the full rate of $52.00 applies if payment is by institutional check, even if the subscription is designated for an individual.) Standing orders are accepted.

Single copies are available at $12.95 when payment accompanies order. (California, New Jersey, New York, and Washington, D.C., residents please include appropriate sales tax.) For billed orders, cost per copy is $12.95 plus postage and handling.

Substantial discounts are offered to organizations and individuals wishing to purchase bulk quantities of Jossey-Bass sourcebooks. Please inquire.

Please note that these prices are for the calendar year 1988 and are subject to change without notice. Also, some titles may be out of print and therefore not available for sale.

To ensure correct and prompt delivery, all orders must give either the *name of an individual* or an *official purchase order number*. Please submit your order as follows:

Subscriptions: specify series and year subscription is to begin.
Single Copies: specify sourcebook code (such as, TL1) and first two words of title.

Mail orders for United States and Possessions, Latin America, Canada, Japan, Australia, and New Zealand to:
　　　Jossey-Bass Inc., Publishers
　　　350 Sansome Street
　　　San Francisco, California 94104

Mail orders for all other parts of the world to:
　　　Jossey-Bass Limited
　　　28 Banner Street
　　　London EC1Y 8QE

New Directions for Teaching and Learning Series
Robert E. Young, *Editor-in-Chief*
Kenneth E. Eble, *Consulting Editor*

TL1　*Improving Teaching Styles,* Kenneth E. Eble
TL2　*Learning, Cognition, and College Teaching,* Wilbert J. McKeachie
TL3　*Fostering Critical Thinking,* Robert E. Young

Contents

Editors' Notes

It is Monday morning. Sue and Karen hurry to take their places at the seminar table, where eight other students are already seated. All of them are liberal arts majors, engaged this semester in part-time internships at sites related to their areas of study. The instructors, representing two different liberal arts disciplines, begin the session by asking students to share problems or opportunities that have arisen in the past week at their sites.

Joan has been at her site, the personnel office of a large company, one day a week for four weeks now. She tries to describe the leadership-development project to which she has been assigned, but she seems frustrated and confused. She is not sure what the project is supposed to accomplish or what she should do. "I've never even taken a course on leadership," she says.

Barbara is puzzled. Again and again, the psychological theories she has been learning in class refuse to fit what she finds at her placement in a home for runaway adolescents. She does not see the clients falling into the categories she has read about in her textbooks, nor are the counselors using any identifiable theories as they work with those clients. Barbara is not sure whether to believe the textbooks or her experience.

Sue is clearly a star among English majors. Faculty members comment on her sensitive analyses of literature, and she contributes regularly to the college literary magazine. She cannot understand what is wrong with her mentors at the public relations firm where she has been placed. "They want me to take all the style and creativity out of my press releases," she moans. "My ideas about good writing just don't match theirs."

These are the kinds of scenes we have encountered every Monday at noon for the past eight years. As instructors of a seminar on off-campus experiential learning required of all liberal arts students at Alverno College, we have heard Joan's and Barbara's and Sue's dilemmas over and over. We have heard them from colleagues across the country as well.

As many faculty members discover, students who excel in difficult theoretical courses can sometimes be surprisingly paralyzed by the working world, while those who rarely contribute in class may come forward with thoughtful, substantive responses to challenges in a professional setting. Many students either lack or do not successfully apply the skills of inquiry and reflection that are needed to derive learning from a situation that, unlike the classroom, is not structured around their needs as learners. Often what they lack is a framework, a set of lenses that will allow them to perceive some pattern and significance in the tasks required at their sites. Other students bring a conceptual framework or theory to bear on work tasks, but they find that it does not correspond to what they see. In response to this discrepancy, they may take a dualistic approach, concluding that one must choose between theory and reality. Again and again, we see instances in which students are not able to link what they know with what they do.

There is a tradition in education of assuming that what is learned in the classroom will make a difference in the larger world of public life and professional work, that classroom learning will somehow connect with or have an impact on students' experiences outside the classroom. What we have seen, however, is that for many students the gap between knowing and doing is large, indeed.

This gap opens with particular force in programs that involve off-campus placements, but what is at issue is not, after all, career preparation. The student who cannot relate what she has learned in Psych 202 to her work with clients at a clinical site is simply a more striking instance of problems that run all through the curriculum. They are easy to spot in students' inability to make connections among courses, apply what they are learning in one class to another, and bring knowledge to bear on particular problems. With these problems comes a set of challenges: *How do we involve students in their learning? How do we overcome passivity in the classroom? How can knowledge be made personal and important for students? How do we help students translate what they know into effective action, now and in the future?*

The echoes here of recent national reports and public pronouncements about higher education are loud and clear, perhaps even somewhat tedious. More noteworthy is the implied epistemological concern: To ask about involvement in learning is also to ask what we mean, anyway, when we say a student knows, what the relationship is between knowing and doing, and what the role of experience is in the kind and level of learning we expect from college students.

In the chapters that follow, these questions are met head on by educators from four quite different settings: a school of engineering; a Washington, D.C., internship program that draws students from a variety of liberal arts disciplines; a university program for "new learning"; and a liberal arts college for women. As practitioners, we seek through our methods, assumptions, and insights to provide an in-depth account of what it means to work with particular students in particular educational contexts—to link knowing and doing. We have aimed not so much for a balance between as a weaving together of theory and practice.

Weaving is an appropriate metaphor for the theme of this volume. Although in very different ways, all the chapters examine how students learn to weave together, to integrate, the pieces of what they know and do. Off-campus programs play some role in several chapters, but other chapters look at strategies that run across the curriculum and are broadly applicable.

Indeed, one principle behind this sourcebook is that off-campus programs differ in degree, not in kind, from learning appropriate to the larger curriculum. True, students do engage in different learning activities off campus; they are, one might argue, more active, and their problems may be more "real," but we believe that students need to demonstrate what they know by actually practicing philosophy, psychology, and chemistry in "real" ways in the classroom as well.

Our argument, then, is that learning by experience needs to occur across the curriculum. A number of issues are bound up in that argument, and it may be helpful to list them here briefly, by way of entrée into the chapters that develop and illustrate them:

- Learning must be active, involving, engaging
- Learning involves not only the cognitive but also other dimensions
- Knowing and doing must be pursued together in an ongoing integrative way, whereby each activity redefines and transforms the other
- Self-reflection, or examination of oneself as a learner, is crucial to linking knowing and doing
- Learning by experience is a concept that must permeate the curriculum in a systematic and developmental way.

Pat Hutchings
Allen Wutzdorff
Editors

Pat Hutchings is director of the Assessment Forum, a project of the American Association for Higher Education. She is on leave from her position as associate professor of English at Alverno College.

Allen Wutzdorff is chair of the Experiential Learning Council at Alverno College and a member of the psychology department.

*Knowing how students learn can help us guide them toward
the integration of their knowledge with experience.*

Experiential Learning Across the Curriculum: Assumptions and Principles

Pat Hutchings, Allen Wutzdorff

Learning through experience is an idea whose time came long ago. Medieval apprentices worked side by side with goldsmiths and masons, and Renaissance painters learned their art by copying and filling in their masters' drawings. Following a long tradition, today's young lawyers clerk for more experienced ones, and beginning doctors practice as interns under resident supervisors. What it means to learn by doing sociology or philosophy or physics, however, is less evident. To what extent does it make sense to talk about learning through experience across the curriculum of a liberal arts institution? What would such a program look like, and on what principles would it effectively operate?

One place to begin looking for answers to these questions is in the work of Dewey (1916). Like many who have recently called for educational reform, Dewey argued that education must be active and involved. Knowledge must be linked to experience, he said, not set apart in "abstract, bookish" forms divorced from life. It must be grounded in "the depth of meaning that attaches to its coming within urgent daily interests" (p. 8). Nevertheless—and here is Dewey's caveat to educators— "mere activity does not constitute experience." Rather, experience

P. Hutchings and A. Wutzdorff (eds.). *Knowing and Doing: Learning Through Experience.*
New Directions for Teaching and Learning, no. 35. San Francisco: Jossey-Bass, Fall 1988.

involves both "trying," an active component, and "undergoing," a passive one. The interaction between these two leads to learning. According to Dewey, "To learn from experience is to make a backward and forward connection between what we do to things and what we enjoy or suffer from things in consequence. Under such conditions, doing becomes a trying, an experiment with the world to find out what it is like; the undergoing becomes instruction—discovery of the connections of things" (p. 140).

For Dewey, knowledge entails a full-bodied involvement or experience with things—for example, the knowing that a concert pianist brings to her performance of a difficult concerto, or the kind captured in the colloquialism, "He really knows his stuff." This chapter argues that this is the kind of learning a liberal education should develop—learning that is personal and active and entails an integration of knowing and doing.

Integrated Learning

Integration may take a variety of forms. A psychology student reads about Freud's theory of sublimation; applying that framework to a simulated therapy setting, she comes to understand it in a deeper, fuller way. A biology student comes to know photosynthesis not only as an abstract concept but also in a concrete, experiential way by conducting experiments in a lab. An English student who is asked to write a Shakespearean sonnet gains a vivid sense of the constraints and possibilities of the form. These are modest examples, but each holds a crucial grain of truth: that doing, or experience, can deepen and extend the nature of knowing.

How does this happen? What is known about the interaction between knowing and doing in the learning process? To begin answering these questions, we can turn to students and listen to what they tell us about how they learn. Every semester, in a seminar for students with off-campus placements, we ask class members to describe and analyze something they learned in the past from direct experience, as opposed to from a text. We discourage them from focusing on too sophisticated an ability, and we suggest examples ranging from roller skating to checkbook balancing. (One semester, to the class's delight, a student wrote about kissing.) The interesting point, regardless of the example, is that as students examine their own and others' learning, they invariably uncover a process that includes several distinct (although not neatly sequential) stages: observation (watching Mother balance her checkbook); actual doing (taking that first step on roller skates); reflection on what has been done, usually at some distance ("It took me five hours to balance my checkbook—there must be a better way"); trial and error (skating with and without arm movements); development of something like a hypothesis or theory that will tell the learner what works, what does not, and what to do next ("Is it possible the bank makes mistakes?"); and, finally, testing of theories through further experience. With this step, the cycle begins again.

It is important to note that this account of how we learn through experience is more than a fancy restatement of the familiar theory-and-practice model: learning Freud, applying Freud; memorizing the Pythagorean theorem, doing twenty problems. As we see it, and as students describe it, the integration of knowing and doing is not simply a matter of application but rather an ongoing interactive process in which both knowledge and experience are repeatedly transformed.

A student who works part-time in a public relations office, for instance, may begin her work on press releases with a certain communications framework in mind, one she learned from a text or a lecture. Finding that her product is less than totally successful, however, she begins modifying that framework, and that action in turn will modify her next piece of work. She will need to find or fashion a framework that suits her personal style, the tasks at hand, and the particular environment. For instance, she may have to modify a personally expressive, "creative" writing style in order to convey information in a crisp, succinct manner that is consistent with the image the office wants to project. Over time, this process of testing and adapting what she knows will help her develop the diverse array of strategies and styles a mature writer can call on—a knowledge that is contextual, nuanced, grounded in experience, and "do-able."

The similarity between, on the one hand, the stories students tell about their learning and, on the other, the models that emerge from learning theory is striking. In their early work, for instance, Argyris and Schön (1974) explored the intersections of knowing and doing. Working with graduate students doing internships, they developed the notion of a theory of action, the set of assumptions, methods, and hypotheses that a professional acquires over time and through experience to tell him or her how to behave in a new situation. This theory of action is itself originally developed through the interaction between an "espoused theory" and a "theory-in-use" (see Figure 1). The espoused theory is the theory with which one enters a situation—the set of assumptions and methods and knowledge one intends to bring to bear. For the history student, it might be a model of analysis based on Marx; for the management major, a faith in management by objectives, as she has learned it from her textbook. The point, of course, is that once in the situation, once we must begin doing something with our espoused theory, a kind of imbalance is created. What we actually do, or what we see afterward that we could have done more effectively (even what we see others doing), Argyris and Schön (1974) call the "theory-in-use," which in turn modifies the original espoused theory, and so on. As indicated by the two-directional arrow in

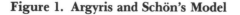

Figure 1. Argyris and Schön's Model

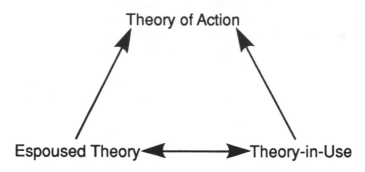

Theory of Action

Espoused Theory ◄─────────► Theory-in-Use

Figure 1, the interaction between the two is ongoing and dialectical. Learning by experience is not simply a matter of applying a theory.

Kolb (1984) also helps us understand the integration of knowledge and experience. Kolb suggests that learning occurs in a variety of modes, from concrete experience to abstract conceptualization, and from reflection to active testing. These categories describe various styles of learning, but they can also be seen as stages in an ongoing cycle of learning that integrates knowing and doing (see Figure 2).

Many educators have been drawn both to Kolb's model and to the work of Argyris and Schön. The conceptual frameworks they set forth help us tell where individual students are in their learning. They help us make sense of what we see in our classrooms—which is, when it comes down to it, what we need to know to do our best as college teachers. Faculty members seeking to incorporate an experiential dimension into the curriculum would do well to begin with work like Argyris and Schön's and Kolb's. Nevertheless, these models will eventually be adapted

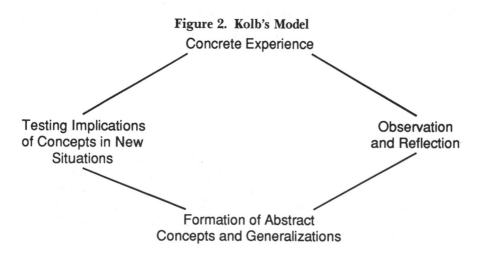

Figure 2. Kolb's Model

Concrete Experience

Testing Implications of Concepts in New Situations

Observation and Reflection

Formation of Abstract Concepts and Generalizations

and adjusted, as they have been at Alverno College, to particular institutional circumstances.

The Alverno College Experiential Learning Model

Alverno College (Milwaukee, Wisconsin) is a liberal arts college for women. Approximately two thousand students pursue degrees in the liberal arts, as well as in nursing, business and management, and education. The curriculum is organized around eight outcomes, which represent both the content and process of liberal learning: effective communications, analytical ability, problem solving, valuing in decision making, social interaction, responsibility toward the global environment, effective citizenship, and esthetic responsiveness. To graduate, students must not only complete the course requirements set forth by their majors but also must demonstrate ability in these eight areas at specified levels of sophistication.

This focus on outcomes is both a source and a consequence of Alverno's efforts to integrate knowing and doing. A key step is rethinking disciplines in terms of outcomes, asking what it means to teach, say, English or history, chemistry, or nursing. Whereas most graduate training aims toward highly specialized knowledge of a small field, teaching at the undergraduate level calls for seeing the content of disciplines in a larger curricular context and in terms of students' overall learning and development.

A more concrete way of putting this—in philosophy, for instance—is to ask how the student will be different as a result of studying Plato, Kant, and Husserl. Certainly, he or she will have some familiarity with the philosophical canon but will also develop certain habits of mind, certain attitudes and abilities inherent in the discipline. (Even more intriguing, one could ask what outcomes would result from studying Plato, but not Kant.) Learning in the discipline, then, is defined in terms of both knowing the content of philosophy and practicing it—thinking and acting like a philosopher. Seen in this way, every discipline entails performance. Moreover, the character of performance changes as students move through their courses of study.

As freshmen, students tend to see knowing and doing as relatively discrete entities (the faculty's urging toward integration notwithstanding); knowing what is in the textbook seems to have little to do with speaking or writing assignments. With sustained effort across the curriculum, however, the dichotomy begins to break down. Students more readily begin to see the applications of the content they are learning. They can test the meaning of their knowledge as they are required to speak and write about it, to connect it to their own experience. In an upward spiral of closer and closer integration, knowing and doing come

Figure 3. Integrated Performance Model

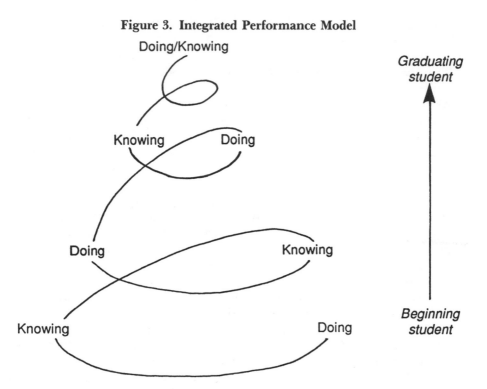

together in performance. Figure 3 shows a "bedspring" model of the way we see students develop over time in an experiential curriculum. How and why does this development take place? Attempting to articulate what we do and why, we have identified four general principles and strategies, discussed in the following sections.

Concreteness

Learning must be rooted in the student's own experience. This dictum may mean either beginning with the experience the student brings to the learning situation or building an experience into that learning. Connecting learning to students' own concrete experience is something good teachers seem to do instinctively. In addition, some disciplines have a history of making learning experiential and concrete. The sciences have long required laboratory work as well as lectures; students learn about photosynthesis or molecular structure both deductively and, in lab experience, inductively. In literature, to begin from concrete experience may mean to teach an abstraction, such as tragedy, inductively: Rather than starting from Aristotle's definition, an action that is serious, complete, and of a certain magnitude, one might begin by asking students what they mean when they use the word *tragic*, teasing out the notion of undeserved and yet perhaps ennobling suffering, and perhaps a sense of irony. From there, one can move to the nuances of tragedy, as defined at various times and in various places. In the case of writing, even fairly unsophisticated students can have gained significant knowledge from their own experience. Asked to think about a time they felt satisfied with something they wrote, and to describe how they wrote it, students will uncover many of the essential points: having a clear sense of audience and purpose, being involved in the subject, using examples, organizing ideas, and so on. What might otherwise seem to be arbitrary, abstract rules can thus be made into concrete personal knowledge with the authority of lived experience behind it.

The power of concreteness to connect knowing and doing is particularly evident in an introductory course on social systems offered by Alverno's sociology department. One way to introduce students to this subject might be to assign readings on social structure, to lecture on theories of how social structure influences groups and individuals, and to discuss such issues with the class. This method certainly could be effective, but the two instructors who have shared responsibility for this course over the past several years have discovered that this deductive method does not always work. They found that students repeated theories but did not apply them to their own experiences and lives. The instructors got the best results by leaving theory until later and beginning with students' experience, and instead of building theories out of air, building theory on that experience. "Rather than assuming all students had experiences relevant to the topic," the instructors report, "we made the class itself the needed experience."

The class works like this: During the first session, students are told to form groups, choose social issues to investigate, and begin work—all with minimal instruction. In the frustration and confusion that inevitably follow, students plunge (or are plunged) directly into the issues the course is most centrally concerned with: how groups select leaders, how social systems make decisions, and how they handle conflict. The instructors intervene only occasionally during the first weeks of the semester, believing that the students' confusion and frustration is a necessary part of the experience and thus a necessary stage in learning these concepts. Assignments during and after the experience ask students to observe and reflect on their own processes in their groups or (in the language of the discipline) in their social systems. Thus, this course, which might easily tend toward abstract theoretical formulations, becomes an experiential laboratory much like one attached to a biology or chemistry course. (Indeed, all courses—not just the sciences, but also art, history, music theory, semantics, and the rest—would arguably benefit from a laboratory component. In the concrete context of the lab, students can engage in experiences that help them generate, test, and transform their knowledge.)

Involvement

The examples already cited suggest another concept behind the successful integration of knowing and doing: Such learning not only is rooted in concrete experience but also involves and engages a range of domains—the cognitive faculties, of course, but also the kinesthetic, affective, ethical, attitudinal, and behavioral dimensions of learning. Learning acquired through several modalities is more likely to "stick," as psychological research has clearly confirmed. Surely, we know this from our own experience as well: We learn more, and more deeply, when learning touches on things that we care about.

Putting the notion of involvement into practice is another matter. Once again, Dewey comes to mind, for the "father of progressive education" was distressed to find classrooms turned into playrooms in the name of greater physical involvement in learning. Many other educators have also had strong feelings about both the feasibility and the appropriateness of holding students accountable for outcomes that have ethical or attitudinal dimensions. On the one hand, how would we know? On the other, it is none of our business. Nevertheless, the notion of involving the whole person in learning calls for serious consideration.

The possibility of kinesthetic learning is a case in point. Aside from scattered requirements for physical education, higher education has left the body behind. Students may be required to play a semester of volleyball, but the possibility that for some students movement might be a powerful learning tool has received short shrift. We are struck by the example of a colleague in the political science department, who uses volleyball and folk dancing to teach, respectively, competition and cooperation—to teach them not just as abstract concepts but also as lived physical and emotional realities. Consider, too, the psychology instructor who teaches the concept of neuron transmission by having students dash between stations (neurons) with messages. They do not, she reports, forget that lesson. In engineering or art history, students may grasp the structural principles behind the flying buttress or the cantilever more vividly by creating those forms with their bodies. In literature, students might dance the shape or structure of a play or poem, giving form to the concepts of tension, climax, and resolution. In a nursing course, a student might spend a day in a wheelchair to know more completely the reality of being handicapped in a society only minimally attentive to special needs. A day in a wheelchair, of course, involves the student not only kinesthetically but in other ways. His or her emotions are called into play, as are values and attitudes about the responsibilities of society to care for the individual, about the meaning of health, and about the relative importance of mind and body. (Most disciplines occasionally call forth these more personal responses.) The question is how to turn per-

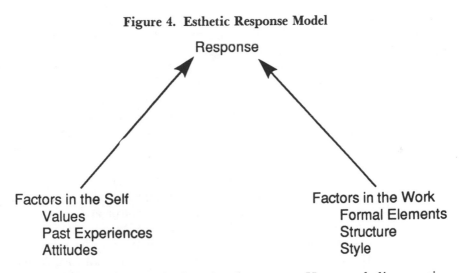

Figure 4. Esthetic Response Model

sonal involvement toward educational purposes. How can feelings, attitudes, and values complement and enrich learning?

Courses in the arts and humanities bring this question into focus. In these disciplines, the significance of the affective domain traditionally has been addressed. Although the formalism of the New Criticism during the middle decades of this century sought to shunt all personal elements of response in favor of (ostensibly) objective analysis of texts, the legitimacy of emotional involvement (which most centuries have taken for granted) has recently been reestablished. Reader-response theories of literature posit that one's understanding of a work of art stems from both its formal structure and from subjective factors brought by the audience to the work: personal experiences, values, feelings, and so forth. The value of integrating objective, formal analysis of a work with subjective response is explicitly set forth in a model of esthetic response employed in an introductory arts and humanities course at Alverno College (see Figure 4).

Ask a beginning student of poetry to articulate his affective response to Alexander Pope, and probably he will not get much beyond "I don't like it; it's boring." Using the model, however, one might ask the student to reflect on that feeling: What is it in the work (heroic couplets? eighteenth-century diction?) that arouses this response? Equally important, what is it in the student (assumptions about the nature of poetry? a romantic sensibility? limited familiarity with prosody?) that makes for boredom?

In a religious-studies course, "Control of Life and Death," we see a different application of the model. As listed in the syllabus, the goals of the course include several cognitive outcomes, including "understanding death as a spiritual and religious event and as a psychological process," but students are also expected "to respond to artistic expressions of human experiences of death and its meaning." The notion of integration is explicit: Students must make personal, cognitive, and affective responses to artistic expressions of death and dying; they must evaluate their personal beliefs and attitudes toward death. Such goals represent a world of feeling, emotion, personal values, and beliefs that is difficult to ignore in the learning process. This is not to deny that such personal involvement is problematic in education; some would even argue that it cannot be taught in the first place. Even granting that it is teachable, what can it mean to require a personal response? Who can tell us how to feel, what to believe? Does a taxonomy of affective development (Krathwohl, Bloom, and Masia, 1964) make any sense? What comes first in, say, looking at a Goya or a Raphael—cognition or affect? How do the two act on each other in learning? Answers to these questions, and their implications for teaching and learning, remain to be answered, yet, the world of personal response is unavoidable. To call for involvement is to assert the role of what Scheffler (1977) refers to as "the cognitive emotions": "Growth of cognition is then, in fact, inseparable from the education of the emotions."

Dissonance

Involving students in their own learning in the ways we have suggested is what makes possible a third strategy for integrating knowing and doing: dissonance, throwing learners temporarily out of balance to move them toward deeper understanding. Frick (1977) makes a useful distinction between quantitative experience (which is cumulative, the result of newer experiences added to previous ones) and qualitative experience (which is instantaneous, with "new information crashing in on old ignorance"). Dissonance may not always do its work so violently, but the urgency and the sense of deep-seated change implied by Frick's metaphor are part of the knowing-doing dialectic.

Once again, the work of Argyris and Schön (1974) comes to mind. Working with students doing field placements, Argyris and Schön postulate the existence of a flexible yet detailed construct from which a professional makes decisions and takes action. This theory of action results from the interplay, indeed the mismatch, between "espoused theory" and "theory-in-use," the former a theoretical framework or set of assumptions, and the latter what one actually does in a particular situation. Nursing students, for example, may enter their clinical experiences with carefully articulated plans for giving each patient time and consideration, attending not only to immediate physical needs but to the whole person. Given the press of many patients and lack of experience, however, they may find themselves doing only urgent, physical tasks. At this point learning occurs, as students attempt to bring "espoused theory" and "theory-in-use" back into balance. In this sense, the theory of action can itself be seen as a dialectic synthesis of what we know and what we do.

This framework proves particularly helpful to students in off-campus internships. The notion of dissonance, or mismatch, between knowing and doing closely matches what they experience. Focusing on points of dissonance—between theory and practice, cognition and emotion, expectation and reality, a "should" and a "must"—students rethink their knowing, reshape their doing, and bring knowledge and action closer and closer together. An Alverno faculty member who mentors off-campus students employs a homelier version of this same principle when she tells students, "If you're comfortable at your site, it's time to change something."

Dissonance may also prompt learning in more traditional settings. A faculty member in the philosophy department finds in dissonance a framework both for understanding students and for pushing their learning ahead. "Sometimes," he says, "students don't understand an idea because they don't like it." Cognition and affect collide. Faced with a world view that violates their own, some otherwise capable students simply cannot engage in appropriate analysis. An obvious example is the student whose strong religious convictions prevent him or her from analyzing the arguments of any philosopher who operates from an atheistic framework. Nevertheless, with careful coaching, the dissonance of this "new information crashing in on old ignorance" (Frick, 1977) can move such a student toward a clearer sense of self and an ability to deal with different perspectives. More unusual are students who "buy" everything, setting aside with apparent ease any conflicting personal views. In this case, a high degree of dissonance may deliberately be invoked, forcing students to confront their own and others' ideas in more fundamental terms and to probe underlying assumptions that otherwise would remain safely submerged and invisible.

Reflection

Related to dissonance, and a key to turning both dissonance and involvement into learning, is reflection, the ability to step back and ponder one's own experience, to abstract from it some meaning or knowledge relevant to other experiences. The capacity for reflection is what transforms experience into learning. The bad news is that reflection, necessary as it is, is not something many students do naturally. Faculty must build into the curriculum occasions that will prompt students to look carefully at their learning and at themselves as learners.

Situations that encourage reflection are often characterized by some degree of distance, which may mean removing a student from a given situation or experience, either through spatial or temporal separation or through affective or cognitive separation. Students can be brought to more and more sophisticated forms of distancing, first if they are required to consider relatively discrete aspects of their learning, and then if they must look across contexts and through time at learning that is more integrated and cumulative.

In an Alverno College seminar for new students, an assignment to write a weekly log requires students to reflect on what and how they are learning in other courses. Throughout the logs, students are asked to write questions about what they have learned in classes each week. (When students proudly announce, "I have no questions," the opportunity is ripe for a short session on types of questions and the relationship between questioning and discovery.) Other sections of the log call on students to make connections between learning in different areas of study ("Describe something you learned in this class this week that changes the way you think about something in another class"), or they may be asked to describe relationships between classroom learning and personal experiences. Connectedness, integration, personal involvement, links between knowledge and experience: These are motifs students encounter even in the first semester at Alverno.

Alverno students first encounter the notion of reflection in the entrance assessment. As part of this assessment, students are asked to demonstrate their speaking ability by preparing a three-minute speech on the topic "Should college be open to everyone who wants to attend, or should admission be based on academic excellence?" Students are given approximately thirty minutes to prepare, and then their speeches are videotaped. As anyone who has undergone this process knows, seeing oneself on videotape is an eye-opener, and it is the ability to look closely at oneself that is actually assessed here. At Alverno, the first level of speaking proficiency lies in the ability to identify from the videotape (with the assistance of a trained observer) one's strengths and weaknesses as a speaker.

During subsequent semesters, four or five longer and increasingly complex speeches are added to the student's permanent videotape. The tape is both an assessment archive for institutional evaluation and, more important, a further prompt for each student to reflect on her own learning. She can look back and find evidence of her growth, as well as of areas where further work is needed.

The value of a longitudinal work sample is also suggested by portfolio-review methods of assessment. At Alverno, for instance, students majoring in the arts and humanities compile portfolios of their work (papers, notes from reading, maps and outlines for oral presentations, taped performances, and so on) from semester to semester. They are encouraged to select samples of their best work but also to include pieces with which they were (or are, in retrospect) less than happy. They are also asked to

Figure 5. Annotated Model of Integrated Performance

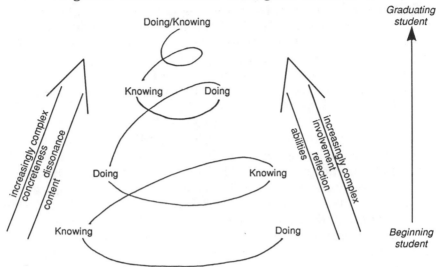

include work from outside the major, so that a philosophy student, for instance, might also include materials from a sociology or management support area.

No doubt the process of selection is itself a prompt for reflection, but students also complete structured analyses of the work they collect, answering questions about repeated themes and interests, patterns of development, strengths, weaknesses, and future goals. The analysis is of the student herself and her learning, a taking stock of her own development. Reflection on an integrated, cumulative sample of work invites her to take an involved and active stance toward her learning and to see it as a lifelong activity in which she is both knower and doer.

Knowing and Doing: Coming Together

It may be helpful to return now to the "bedspring" model of integration, annotating it to reflect the four principles and strategies just discussed (see Figure 5). Concreteness, involvement, dissonance, and reflection: These are principles that characterize and run all through the experiential curriculum, strategies that allow students to bring knowing and doing into increasingly greater integration.

These principles shape the entire curriculum at Alverno, yet at every college or university and in every curriculum there can be "teachable moments," in which integration occurs with particular force. At Alverno, such moments might take place during a semester of off-campus experiential learning, or during the "performance" in which each student participates at the end of the sophomore year (a half-day simulation that assesses and diagnoses the degree to which she brings together knowing and doing through group interaction, speaking, reading, problem solving, and analysis brought to bear on a complex social and political situation). As usual, the student must reflect on her own performance (she must self-assess), but she is also evaluated and given feedback by an external assessor, one of dozens of local professionals (many of them alumnae) who volunteer their services. We call this assessment the "Integrated Competence Seminar."

Each student in the seminar is asked to take her responsibility as a citizen seriously. As a member of the Citizens' Advisory Council, she has the task of formulating guidelines for the selection of books for high school libraries and classrooms. The council must reach consensus on a set of guidelines, which they will forward as recommendations to the board of education of Oakwood, Wisconsin.

The board of education provides the council with several examples of typical complaints about textbooks. Council members also receive reports and position papers, which take a formal look at some of the issues.

On the day of the seminar, each student is given data and background information. She must assimilate it, analyze it, and reorganize it for use throughout the day in a series of experiences. Her first task is to study a set of communications typical of the demands made on her as a member of the council. These items all require some kind of response or action. Her second task is to give a speech, stating and supporting her position on a particular issue of textbook controversy. Finally, she meets with the other members of the council to formulate guidelines and policies for recommendation to the board of education. Both this meeting and her speech are videotaped. The student ends the day with an interview that reviews her experience.

When the day is over, the student is asked to review and evaluate her own performance. At the same time, a team of assessors carefully reviews the materials, written and oral, that she has produced. The assessment team reaches consensus on the strengths the student has shown in the situation. The student then receives oral feedback, which describes and interprets her performance in the seminar so that she can understand her strengths and weaknesses. She also receives a written statement summarizing the feedback. This statement provides direction for the student, as well as for the faculty of her major department, in planning her academic program.

The strategies discussed earlier in this chapter all appear and come together here, in the Integrated Competence Seminar. The assessment draws out and examines learning in a concrete, experiential setting. The student is active and involved—making decisions, speaking, and taking a stance based on analysis of the situation and on her own values and attitudes. Because conflicting viewpoints come forth at several points, dissonance may become a factor.

Reflection is also a key motif. The use of videotape and the final interview both distance the student from her own participation, thus allowing her to have more reflective judgment of her strengths and weaknesses. Moreover, feedback from an external assessor—an individual who brings what is literally an outside perspective—helps the student see herself through other eyes.

Ultimately, the integration of knowing and doing is a movement toward self-assessment: the capacity to be involved but objective, to make connections, and to generalize. A number of effects can be inferred from experiential learning. Most important, perhaps, is the ability to learn from experience.

References

Argyris, C., and Schön, D. *Theory in Practice: Increasing Professional Effectiveness.* San Francisco: Jossey-Bass, 1974.

Dewey, J. *Democracy and Education.* Toronto, Ont.: Macmillan, 1916.

Frick, S. "Toward a Definition of Experience." *Liberal Education,* 1977, *63,* 495–499.

Kolb, D. *Experiential Learning: Experience as the Source of Learning and Development.* Englewood Cliffs, N.J.: Prentice-Hall, 1984.

Krathwohl, D. R., Bloom, B., and Masia, B. *Taxonomy of Educational Objectives.* Vol. 2. *Affective Domain.* New York: McKay, 1964.

Scheffler, I. "In Praise of the Cognitive Emotions." *Teachers College Record,* 1977, *79,* 171–186.

Pat Hutchings is director of the Assessment Forum, a project of the American Association for Higher Education. She is on leave from her position as associate professor of English at Alverno College.

Allen Wutzdorff is chair of the Experiential Learning Council at Alverno College and a member of the psychology department.

*Engineering colleges have not been known for their national
leadership in liberal education. An experiment, which started
in 1972 and affected the entire curriculum of a college, may
change all that.*

Liberal Learning in Engineering Education: The WPI Experience

*William R. Grogan, Lance E. Schachterle,
Francis C. Lutz*

In the late 1960s, a core of senior engineering faculty at Worcester Polytechnic Institute (WPI), a long-established college graduating about five
hundred professional majors annually, proposed a reevaluation of the
entire curriculum of the college. These colleagues examined the ferment
of educational change taking place around them, considered the wide-
spread fears that technology was blighting America and the world, and—
thinking about their own careers—assessed the factors that promoted real
dedication to teaching, learning, and responsible professions. They con-
cluded that conventional classroom teaching, with routine submission of
homework, rewarded short-term performance but failed to provide a last-
ing synthesis of learning. They also recognized that such conventional
technical coursework failed to raise issues of the responsibilities appropriate to students aspiring to enter the professions.

To solve these problems, the WPI faculty curriculum committee proposed an entirely new program based on experiential learning through
projects. Since engineering involves systems of components that cannot
be designed or developed in isolation, course-based engineering pro-

P. Hutchings and A. Wutzdorff (eds.). *Knowing and Doing: Learning Through Experience.*
New Directions for Teaching and Learning, no. 35. San Francisco: Jossey-Bass, Fall 1988.

grams, concentrating necessarily on specific disciplines, fail to provide significant integrating experience. Similarly, to nurture the development of professional values would require immersion in real-world issues going beyond conventional classroom pedagogy.

The Challenge

Engineering students at WPI and elsewhere share certain characteristics. They are academically bright, particularly in mathematics and science. They are used to working hard, in and out of school. Often they are first- or second-generation college students, propelled into college by family hopes that energetic sons and daughters will secure professional positions inaccessible to working-class parents. Oriented toward discipline and a diet of demanding homework, these engineering students tend to accept conventional programs, with the steps toward the degree locked into place by traditions of problem solving and memory-grid teaching.

Engineering classrooms in the 1960s rarely encountered reformist cries for "back to basics," since so few challenges were made that the basics had been forgotten in those classrooms. Such conventional programs, however, risked stagnation, for graduates were ill prepared to deal with nontechnical professionals and with the rapid pace of change they would soon encounter on the job. Engineering education in the 1960s mastered the post–World War II conversion from practicum to rigorous science and mathematical formulation, but students remained passive recipients of this sophisticated wisdom, too often uninterested in their education beyond the next exam. WPI faculty—soon to be joined by the administration, alumni, and students—recognized the weaknesses of this conventional system, which purchased success by rewarding the passive accommodations of students to basic rote work.

The practice of engineering does not depend on turning in homework, but on completing projects on time. Such projects require not only mastery of the technical disciplines but also a command of scheduling, teamwork, and communication skills. Further, few engineers remain strictly within their original disciplines after a decade or so. Successful practitioners move into management and must work and compete with liberal arts and law. Engineers also must offer leadership in technology and in its public use. Engineering education required new thinking about the engagement of students in lifelong learning and their preparation for leadership and social responsibility.

In the 1960s, many undergraduate engineering programs required modest upper-level project work, usually associated with advanced courses or honors. To engage the full personal energy of students as individual learners and future colleagues, WPI proposed a new program, making project activity both a major vehicle for learning and a measure of success in preparing for further study or entry-level employment. Thus, projects moved from the status of honors electives to becoming the focus of the entire undergraduate program, affecting everything from the academic calendar to faculty load.

This chapter describes the background of the WPI experiential program, how it was established, and how it currently operates. Over ten thousand alumni have graduated under the requirements of the program, making possible an analysis and evaluation of its success.

Weaknesses of the Conventional Program

Why, in 1970, WPI found it politically possible to abandon its comfortable, traditional approach to education and create a new project-based curriculum could be the subject of a book itself. There was no crisis, not even administrative pressure. Among the faculty, however, a gnawing dissatisfaction focused on the way the rigidity of the traditional curriculum sapped students' motivation. Science and engineering students were so constrained by the dictates of an inflexible, impersonal system that their development as thoughtful individuals was difficult to achieve. Faculty who followed the careers of their graduates sensed a distressing discontinuity between the students' overall preparation and the actual expectations they faced as young professionals.

No one ever questioned the need for a firm foundation in science and engineering fundamentals. Beyond this base of knowledge, however, a number of paradoxes were increasingly evident. First, a rigid, academic program offers few opportunities for students to assume responsibility for defining their personal objectives, but students' success after graduation depends on this ability. Second, WPI courses, by their nature, usually presented knowledge in long, isolated corridors, but professional achievement requires extensive integration and application of knowledge. Third, classroom experience at WPI was basically passive, but career development requires self-activation. Fourth, the formal classes treated students as isolated learners, but practice involves personal interactions, shared experiences, mutual understanding, and effective communication. Finally, the academic community is inherently a somewhat cloistered environment, but WPI's concentration on science and engineering took it even farther from the world of social involvement.

With these things in mind, the WPI faculty confronted the need to devise an integrated educational system that, while continuing to develop an essential base of engineering knowledge, would require students to synthesize information, transfer ideas from one environment to another, communicate effectively, formulate approaches to complex problems, locate new information, develop self-confidence, and understand other people and their priorities.

Creating a New Approach

To meet the challenge, a comprehensive approach to engineering education was developed and translated into action through a new program, which became known as the WPI Plan. The program was based on some quite new assumptions:

- The integrative needs of engineering education cannot be met exclusively through classroom techniques
- Exemplary objectives may appear in college goals statements, but they do not mean anything to undergraduates unless they are clearly translated into degree requirements
- For undergraduates to benefit from increased involvement, they must be free to make mistakes, acknowledge them, and use them as a basis of further learning
- Academic support systems and faculty attitudes must complement new degree requirements
- Educational activities outside of the traditional classroom are faculty-intensive and sometimes expensive.

New Degree Requirements. All previous academic requirements at WPI were eliminated. In their place, the faculty adopted four new degree requirements:

1. A qualifying project dealing with a problem in one's major field of study, called the Major Qualifying Project, or MQP (quarter-year equivalent)

2. A qualifying project relating science and technology to social concern and human needs, called the Interactive Qualifying Project, or IQP (quarter-year equivalent)

3. A "sufficiency," or minor, in an area of the humanities (five thematically related courses capped by a humanities qualifying project equivalent to one course—the equivalent of half a year's work)

4. Assessment of background fundamentals in mathematics, science, and elementary engineering practice within the major. Since 1987, this assessment has been met by broad distribution requirements, which have replaced a week-long competency examination in the major field. This examination proved inequitable in management and inadequate for ensuring both comprehension of basic principles and their sophisticated application to significant problems.

Building the Support System. With this new approach to learning established, the academic infrastructure was revised accordingly. Changes included altering the calendar from two semesters to four seven-week terms and implementing this wholesale recasting by restructuring over 450 courses. To stimulate project teamwork in an atmosphere of peer support, the faculty instituted a grading system that would not result in grade-point averages. Faculty-load models were devised to reflect the new mix of project and classroom teaching modes. Finally, to oversee the massive revision of the entire undergraduate program, a new post—dean of undergraduate studies—was created. Reporting to the dean was an associate dean who managed the details of supervising 1,300 students in projects each year. A division of interdisciplinary affairs, also reporting to the dean, provided the administrative basis and intellectual home of interdisciplinary studies, including the new IQP.

The Major Qualifying Project (MQP). Although most students at WPI major in one of the four engineering programs (chemical, civil, electrical, and mechanical), bachelor's degrees are also awarded in the sciences (biology and biotechnology, chemistry, and physics), mathematical sciences, and computer science. Other degree-granting programs are offered in management and management engineering. Far fewer students major in WPI's society-technology or humanities-technology programs and in such interdisciplinary programs as environmental planning, but all students do complete the MQP.

No matter what the major, the MQP should provide a culminating experience in the discipline, develop self-confidence, enhance communication skills, and ensure the synthesis of fundamental concepts. In chemistry, these goals are commonly achieved in the laboratory, where scientific inquiry is blended with technology to encourage the examination of advancing theory. In management, projects are likely to involve one or more aspects of the increasing role that technology plays in modern production. In mathematics, theoretical theses explore graph theory, the motion of stellar systems, actuarial analyses, and many other topics. Depending on students' priorities, topics may tend toward in-depth laboratory research or toward the complex problems of designing or producing better products by balancing needs and constraints.

Some MQP experiences put major emphasis on analytical skills, as in the development of a finite-element model of a structural component or in the thermal and kinetic analysis of a chemical process. This diversity of opportunities available to students is a strength of the program and allows tailoring of learning experiences to the educational needs and individual interests of students. *Innovations,* WPI's annual publication of MQP abstracts, distributed free, provides a sense of this diversity.

Diversity is also a barrier, however, to the task of conveying some of WPI's specific educational characteristics to an interested audience of readers. Because the vast majority of WPI's students are engineering majors, and because design is so integral a part of the engineer's experience, we will focus on engineering-design projects for examples of the substantive experience of the MQP.

Design Experiences in the MQP. The most fundamental ability of an engineer is design. Other important abilities include research, project development and management, analysis, justification, and communication. Any course or program intended to provide in-depth appreciation of engineering must have the flexibility to develop these abilities in students and must motivate students to draw from what they learn in other courses. At WPI, the faculty chose to implement such integration through the MQP, which is equivalent to a quarter-year of full-time activity. The MQP provides a capstone design experience. The term *capstone* refers to the extended application and synthesis of the scientific, mathematical, and engineering principles previously learned in the foundation of the curriculum.

Engineering design is the process of preparing and carrying out a plan to accomplish something; it is a means to an end. It is not pure artistic creativity, nor is it the rote application of codes or algorithms. The essence of engineering design is the pursuit of appropriate solutions, applying what can be thought of as skilled art, built on a foundation of technical knowledge and engineering science.

Problems assigned to students in traditional coursework are almost always carefully structured. Thus, there is little room for variation in the path to a solution. Students become adept at solving such problems, and most educational programs are founded on the use of solution methodologies, varying only in the discipline and level of difficulty. A good design experience, in contrast, immediately causes consternation, as students come to realize their well-developed problem-approach techniques do not work. The problem is too big. It involves unfamiliar disciplines, there is an unwieldy number of defined and undefined parameters, and no single correct solution exists.

As a process, engineering design eludes prescription. In addressing unstructured problems such as those encountered in design, algorithmic thought processes must be augmented by intellectual reasoning of a different type. This step is difficult for most students. First, they must define the problem in descriptive terms acceptable to the project team. This step is difficult because, in engineering education, problems are usually predefined; thus, students have little experience in problem definition. Second, students need to identify the key elements of the problem, those that must be addressed, as opposed to those of little consequence. Most students have no such experience. Third, the key elements, once identified, must be the subject of an intense application of engineering principles. Students often believe that design is an art somehow not subject to such fundamentals. Finally, the process should be iterated, to make the key elements more compatible and gradually bring lower-priority elements into the design. Through this process, various means to achieve the goal are synthesized.

The space environment, as an example, is a particularly rich source of diverse design problems for MQPs. WPI has been fortunate in securing corporate and NASA cooperation in developing several ongoing MQP activities in space design and engineering. Some examples of recent MQPs dealing with engineering design in the space environment include student participation in a national competition to produce an improved spacesuit glove, and the production of several experiments to be flown on a future space-shuttle mission. (Descriptions of these projects are available through the WPI Projects Office.) Like so many others, these projects have brought to the curriculum a mechanism for motivating students, a problem-solving environment requiring a balance between idealism and practicality, and a capacity for developing self-confidence that grows out of dealing with open-ended complexity.

These conditions of engineering design are sometimes brought to mind by the phrase *real-world problems*. Engineering education draws on the experience of faculty to bring students this essential element of engineering practice. Design, however, is much more than experiential decision making. It also requires the application of technical knowledge and skills at a fundamental level. What students know must be translated into, and tested against, what they can do with what they know.

The Interactive Qualifying Project (IQP). In addition to the capstone design experience of the MQP, the WPI Plan stresses both course and project work in the humanities and social sciences; all science and engineering students, to graduate from WPI, must consider the social impact of their professional careers in technology. To complement separate course requirements in the humanities and the social sciences, the faculty has created the IQP, a unique project-based degree requirement.

The IQP requires all students to define, investigate, and report on a topic of their choice that raises questions about the social and human values associated with specific technologies. The IQP is a project, not a series of courses (although students are encouraged to use course requirements in the humanities and social sciences to prepare for the IQP). Like the MQP, the IQP requires the equivalent in effort of at least three courses. Students may work in teams, concentrating their effort in a single term or spreading it over one year (typically, the junior year), and selecting topics from those offered by faculty or external agencies, as well as proposing their own.

Of course, WPI was not the only American institution to seek experimental and experiential models for teaching greater awareness of professional responsibilities. For example, many universities and colleges, particularly those with technical specialties, introduced new courses in professional ethics and in the spectrum of interdisciplinary activities called science, technology, and society (STS). STS programs typically use the humanities (especially history) and the social sciences (especially sociology and policy studies) to examine the foreseen and unforeseen consequences of technology for society. WPI faculty learned from these experiments, and STS studies remain active on the campus. Because the

IQP is project based, however, it differs significantly in three ways from most STS programs.

First, students can define the interaction between science and/or technology and society in many different ways, not all of which would be recognized as STS themes. The majority of students do in fact use the social sciences, especially history and economics, to provide the linking methodologies by which the impact of technology on society is assessed. Nevertheless, students are free to explore the sociotechnological nexus through the arts (such as in projects to improve science education in the schools or employ technology to assist the handicapped).

Second, the IQP is a project, not a series of courses. The designers of the WPI Plan felt strongly that project activity was pedagogically superior to coursework in that projects engaged students in planning and executing activities they had chosen themselves, as opposed to students' taking the more passive role of receiving faculty-dispensed wisdom in required courses.

Third, the IQP is required of every WPI student, above and beyond eight courses in humanities and social sciences. The IQP is neither an honors program nor an elective among alternatives to the humanities/ social science requirements mandated by engineering professional societies.

Interdisciplinary project-based education has its drawbacks, most notably the lack of familiarity with fundamentals that students bring to their projects. Still, WPI faculty believed engineering students would be motivated to learn concepts outside their fields (such as cost-benefit analysis) if they perceived such concepts as necessary to required projects.

For well over a decade, every WPI student has pursued the IQP as a major activity. Thus, almost half of WPI's living graduates have completed IQPs. The best way to understand the IQP is to consider some examples, and the best source of examples is the annual WPI publication *Interactions,* which, like *Innovations,* is available through the WPI Projects Office. *Interactions* lists the abstracts of all IQPs completed in the previous academic year, as well as longer reviews of exemplary projects. More recently, *Interactions* has begun publishing case studies of new programs, such as those offered by the Solar Electronics and Related Technologies Center, and has presented other WPI initiatives in STS studies, such as a new series in science, technology, and culture.

The college sponsors an annual competition, with a selection committee chaired by the president, to select the best IQPs from the previous year. The three 1987 winners, with their abstracts, were the following:

Implementation of a Patient Education Research Center
at the San Francisco General Hospital

Patients leaving the controlled environment of a hospital need information to care for themselves, whether their condition be surgical or medical. Two electrical engineering students formed [the] Patient Education Resource Center at the hospital. Using marketing techniques from management, they designed the patient information with both consumer (patient) and provider (physician) in mind, to [en]sure that the material (information) would be easy to acquire, understand, and use.

Hazardous Waste Sites Cleanup Under Superfund

Working with the National Association of Manufacturers in Washington, D.C., three students examined the technology of disposing of hazardous wastes and considered the conflicts [among] corporations, local governments, and landowners. They reviewed current public policy on cleanups and focused on three of the most notorious sites, recommending ways of implementing quicker cleanups.

Environmental Considerations and Waste Planning on the Lunar Surface

This project examined the legal, environmental, and technical considerations of developing energy and waste disposal resources on the moon. After making some estimates of the size of a lunar base, the student examined in detail alternative energy sources, methods of processing resources for life support and for commercial development, and needs for waste disposal. The report considered these plans in light of present and possible future international agreements on the use of the moon.

These are only three of over three hundred projects conducted in a typical year. As prize winners, they represent the best efforts of our students. In recent years, as the IQP program has matured, the college has undertaken closer assessment of projects to identify and solve the problems associated with weaker projects. Close assessment of IQPs carried out by a faculty peer-review process in the last two summers has disclosed that the large majority of projects fulfill most of the original objectives of the IQP.

The major weakness of past projects has been the emphasis on doing, as opposed to thinking. For example, some students feel more comfortable providing actual social services or writing manuals, as opposed to analyzing social needs or exploring the implications of new technologies. Experiential activities continue to be a valued component of many IQPs, but in fifteen years' experience, faculty have learned how to enhance the learning in many IQPs by insisting that students conduct formal project proposals to delineate the objectives of activities before they begin. Such proposals, like the professional ones that will be encountered later in industry, stress a literature review, in which students assess how well what they propose to do has already been done. This research both sharpens their library skills and enables them to extend work previously done in IQPs and in professional circles. Students who propose, for example, to introduce new computer-teaching aids into slow learners' classrooms would be expected to review in detail the literature on teaching this category of special education, as well as on software prepared for such students. Requirements like this ensure more complete integration of knowledge and experience.

Project Centers and IQP Programs. To encourage students to select IQP topics from real-world situations and needs, early in the program the college began an organized solicitation of project topics from off-campus sponsors. In return for students' efforts on projects, sponsors are expected to designate liaisons to work with student teams—that is, to supply office space, supplies, and communication support if needed, and occasionally to offer modest, direct financial support of projects.

Most important, sponsors must ensure the academic quality and substance of projects. For example, sponsors are asked not to consider students for such repetitive tasks as data entry, but more as consultants working on professional tasks or issues. Sponsors recognized very early that a three-student team working over a seven-week term can produce about one thousand hours of effort and make a significant contribution to an agency's missions. Subsequent professional recruitment of good students is another benefit of these projects for the sponsors.

The structure for supporting off-campus projects has matured effectively in the last decade. Beginning in 1974, WPI began sending students and their faculty advisers to Washington, D.C. to conduct IQPs with federal agencies and national professional and educational institutions. Students have recently completed IQPs on such topics as why many independent inventors do not pay the newly introduced renewal fees required to keep patents active (a project carried out with the U.S. Patent and Trademark Office) and how state legislation affects regulation of nuclear energy facilities (with the American Society for Mechanical Engineers).

The success of the Washington project center led in 1986 to the creation of a parallel center in London, where students conduct similar projects with British agencies. In 1987, WPI students compiled a manpower-prediction survey (with the Institution of Electrical Engineers), examined similarities and differences between patent searches in the British and European patent offices, and assisted a guild in a study to improve its award competition for British technological innovations.

These two programs are open to all WPI students (normally juniors); three-person teams are selected by competitions, which include interviews. The students live in Washington or London for seven weeks, where the sole academic mission is to complete their projects. In the quarter before they leave campus, they complete preliminary work to ensure that they have the background and conceptual tools to complete projects successfully. This preparation culminates in formal project proposals that are discussed in detail with agency liaisons to reduce any misunderstandings about projects' objectives. WPI faculty who advise projects participate in project proposals and accompany students to the off-campus sites to provide support and advice while the students carry out their projects.

These examples notwithstanding, most students continue to carry out their projects closer to home. In 1986, WPI launched two centers for projects with off-campus agencies in and around Worcester. The Center for Municipal Studies, led by an electrical engineer with a strong interest in citizen participation in local government, offers projects to assist local government agencies by providing teams of engineering students to address appropriate issues. One team, for example, studied the technology and cost benefits of using a municipal cable system for metering and billing users for electricity. Another team wrote a computer program to help in the management of Worcester's public works department.

The Center for Solar Electrification also works with students on campus, although these projects may take students part of the time to the New England mountains to study the advantages of solar PV electricity for remote sites, or even to the Third World to consider the social and economic impact of using solar PV as an energy source in communities that have never had service from a central grid. Students also have done projects on public education concerning the advantages of PV power generation.

Other established programs based on campus involve technology and special education, the Worcester Juvenile Court, and "living museums" (projects carried out with regional museums). As the faculty's interests coalesce around topics that promise significant opportunities, new centers are formed. Recently the college announced two new initiatives: the Center for School-College Collaboration in Science and Math Education, and the Center for Values, Health Care, and Technology. The first center will bring together students and faculty engaged in a spectrum of project activity on education, including work with minorities and special-education pupils. The second center provides an umbrella for IQPs that are conducted both locally and through several San Francisco hospitals and that focus on the social and ethical issues emerging from the application of new technologies.

Faculty Roles and Administrative Structures

When WPI initiated the IQP program, all faculty were considered as potential advisers, not just those from departments or fields (mainly the social sciences) where relevant disciplinary expertise could be assumed. The senior faculty who devised the IQP concept were persuaded that engineering students would participate most effectively in sociotechno-

logical projects if they could see engineering faculty willing to risk stretch-
ing their own expertise to be advisers and include the topics appropriate
to IQPs. Social-science faculty were welcomed as advisers, coadvisers, and
mentors to nonsocial-science faculty but were by no means expected to be
involved with every IQP on campus.

Whatever advantages this strategy had for inducing engineering students to follow their disciplinary faculty into interdisciplinary projects,
the disadvantages were obvious. Engineering faculty had no special skills
in advising IQP projects—beyond, perhaps, personal experience as project managers and some awareness of technologies with potentially important social consequences. Locating the advising pool for IQPs outside a
formal STS or social-science faculty had advantages for integrating the
IQP into the fabric of the college's mission but also raised the danger of
guidance by enthusiastic but uninformed advisers.

When the college undertook the responsibility of requiring an interactive project of every student, drawing sharp distinctions around the
definition of the IQP was unwise. The first concern was simply to offer
topics sufficient to sustain this novel degree requirement. Consequently,
for the first several years, students and faculty accepted as IQPs a diversity
of possible themes and topics. Social-sciences faculty, on and off campus,
participated in summer institutes to make their colleagues aware of the
kinds of social-science skills students would find useful in doing IQPs.

This creative ferment was exciting. Students participated in the early
project centers off campus. They recorded, edited, and analyzed the Water-
gate hearings. They designed production boards for plays and wrote
autobiographical novels about becoming engineers. They gathered and
interpreted information about responses to issues of nuclear power, based
on differences in gender, major, and college choice. They assessed the
economic and environmental impacts of new and old energy sources and
tried new ways of teaching mathematics and the sciences in the public
schools.

In these ventures, the faculty learned along with the students, often
prompted by the need to stay one step ahead of bright, inquiring, active
minds. Administration of the program was coordinated through the Division for Interdisciplinary Affairs (or DIA), but IQP advising was the
responsibility of all faculty; it was not confined to a single group.
Enough established faculty in engineering were willing to learn how to
advise or coadvise IQP projects, or to listen to colleagues in other disciplines, to make the new program work.

Long-term commitment to the IQP as a degree requirement, however,
made some degree of "routinization of charisma" a necessity. A faculty
trio composed of colleagues in humanities, social sciences, and engineering assessed ongoing faculty interest in IQP advising and observed that
long-term faculty commitment to IQP's fell into eleven broad categories:

technology and environment, energy and resources, health care and technology, regional studies and planning, science and technology policy and management, social studies of science and technology, risk analysis and liability, humanistic studies of technology, economic growth and stability and development, social and human services, and education in a technological society.

Each of these areas has a coordinator (and, in some cases, two) to oversee projects. Moreover, projects submitted in fulfillment of the IQP requirement are reviewed annually. This review process, extensively pursued in the last two years, has established a set of benchmark expectations for IQP advising. The division structure, with its internal peer-review mechanism, lends formal coherence to the IQP division structure. At the same time, the formal divisions have begun to create groups of colleagues with a shared interest in making part of their faculty development involve participation in the IQP. In the 1970s, the college obtained external support for its new program and had resources for summer seminars to bring established faculty into IQP advising. More recently, with WPI's growing concern for research, the division structure has played an important role in identifying topics that newer faculty can explore as possible themes for IQP advising.

Since the college adopted the WPI Plan, the number of faculty and students involved has grown considerably. The department of social science, as well as the humanities department, with its six-course service requirement, have expanded, yet the IQP has remained an obligation of all faculty. The eleven thematic areas provide not only interdisciplinary themes that focus the attention of established faculty for IQP advising, but also topics that allow new faculty to probe their own interests.

Over half of full-time faculty now advise IQPs. No single department has special duties to promote interdisciplinary teaching or research. Faculty participation in the IQP program remains voluntary, yet the disciplinary balance—among engineering, science, management, social sciences, and humanities—remains healthy. Students have abundant opportunities for topics; many more are suggested by faculty than students can select.

Further Integration: The Humanities

As the Interactive Qualifying Project program took shape, it became increasingly clear to faculty that integration was a powerful educational concept, one that warranted further attention, particularly in the humanities.

Dissatisfied with the superficial traditional approach to the humanities in its science and engineering programs, the college established the humanities sufficiency. This degree requirement became the core of the college's commitment to the humanities as an integral part of the education of scientists and engineers. The requirement assumes an attitude on the part of students and faculty that is quite different from the traditional obeisance to humanistic study found in many engineering programs.

The humanities and social-science sectors of engineering curricula have mostly been exercises in educational tokenism. Undercut by some engineering faculty, often taught as a perpetual introductory-level exercise by the hapless faculty assigned to the task, approached by students with the comforting expectation that the experience would not drain their energies, the nontechnical part of an engineering education was an appropriate candidate for reconsideration.

A major conclusion reached at WPI was that a collective humanities and social-science (HSS) requirement—still prevalent elsewhere today—could not adequately address the situation. Accordingly, two distinct requirements were established: the IQP, plus two social-science courses; and the humanities sufficiency. In the humanities, a second major decision was reached: Thematic depth was to take precedence over introductory-level breadth. The depth areas included in the sufficiency are language, music, drama, literature, art, philosophy, and history.

The sufficiency could be affiliated with the IQP, as appropriate, and in such areas as ethics and social history some impressive links have been made; the "living museums" program is a prime example.

Perhaps the best way to illustrate the nature of the sufficiency itself is to list examples of actual course sequences and terminal research topics:

Courses: History of Technology
European Technological Development
American Science and Technology to 1859
American Science and Technology from 1859
Science, Technology, and Society

Research Topic: Yorktown and Gettysburg: A Comparative Study of Strategy, Tactics, and Technology

Courses: History of Technology
Concepts in Philosophy and Religion
Religion and Social Ethics
Religions of the World
Religions of the East

Research Topic: The Engineer as a Whistle Blower

The humanities sufficiency has been one of the most successful components of the WPI program. Not only do students cover significant humanistic material, they also develop positive, confident attitudes, as many discover with enthusiasm that they can accomplish serious work in the humanities. In addition, a renewed and strong humanities faculty has been heavily involved in the development and operation of the IQP. The IQP would not have attained the status it enjoys today without the lively involvement of the humanities faculty, and WPI would not have had this type of faculty without the humanities sufficiency requirement.

Implications

Support structures of the college were revised to accommodate the WPI Plan. The faculty found that recasting the academic program so thoroughly required wholesale reexamination of other aspects of college life and experience. First, faculty attitudes toward students, teaching, and the role of their own expertise had to be reconsidered. WPI adopted new course structures, grading systems, advising policies, and even a new calendar and academic-load model.

Faculty. For most of the faculty who were professionally active, the projects posed no great concern. They naturally adapted their professional expertise to the formation and guidance of project activities. They were comfortable with the expected interaction with external organizations, which was to become a major ingredient in the program. There were others, however, who felt threatened by the idea of working with undergraduates in the less formal project environment. They were uncomfortable with a situation in which, after project work had begun, they would be colearners with undergraduates.

Special workshops were organized on the techniques of project management—how, for instance, to help students set objectives that are neither trival nor impossible. It was difficult for some faculty to let students conduct their own projects and make their own mistakes. Conversely, it was also necessary to learn how to provide students with appropriate support while maintaining an appropriate degree of distance and objectivity.

In all this work questions of faculty compensation are inevitable. Indeed, a matter of significant concern to faculty everywhere is how personal contributions to the educational system will be recognized and rewarded. With such a large amount of project activity, the customary unit of "contact hours" does not adequately measure faculty load. Therefore, a new unit, course-student equivalent, was developed, allowing project advising to be integrated with course teaching to produce a faculty-load model. Without such recognition of project advising, the entire effort probably would not have survived.

The Calendar. To better accommodate projects, the semester calendar, with its five or so concurrent course activities, was modified to consist of two seven-week terms, each with three concurrent activities. It was felt that the desired level of project accomplishment would be difficult to attain if projects had to compete with four or five structured courses, all with specific assignments, quiz deadlines, and the like. Once the project became one of three activities, project activity achieved a kind of critical mass.

Grades. The WPI Plan, with its emphasis on teamwork, required a supportive student environment where peer teaching and learning would be encouraged to the fullest degree. Raising expectations for students demands a parallel increase in support levels. Such a cooperative atmosphere is especially important in project work, where the majority of projects involve two or three students. To remove the concern that often arises about class rank and the resulting competition, the college abandoned its former grading system and does not now produce class rankings. The system now uses grades of A, B, C, and NR (No Record, for work that is unsatisfactory).

The change in grading emphasis has had desirable results: Greater mutual support is apparent among students, and qualifying projects, with their abstracts prominently displayed on transcripts, have assumed the primary role intended for them in indicating students' abilities and accomplishments. Without a grade of A in at least one project, for example, it is impossible for a student to graduate with honors. Moreover, project accomplishment is now used as an exclusive measure in evaluating graduates for career placement; after initial resistance, recruiters have learned to assess students more validly by examining project experience. Successful interviewers have learned to review students' projects as if they represented the applicants' first professional experiences. Project-based graduates are often treated as if they were candidates from competitors, rather than college students.

Evaluation

In its project program, WPI has a coherent, experiential curriculum. The two large-scale projects, through which all students must qualify for graduation, draw on the entire campus community for role models and advisers. The MQP and IQP engage students and faculty in real-world problems provided by off-campus programs and agencies. The humanities sufficiency provides a means by which engineering students can cultivate lifelong interests in the humanities or the arts.

In the senior year, the MQP draws students into unusually close contact with faculty in their major fields and provides experiences as valuable as first-year job activity or independent research in graduate school. Employers report that WPI students can move quickly into managerial positions on research teams. In fact, many companies indicate that they treat WPI entry-level students as personnel already experienced in first jobs and more able than most new graduates to move into productive research.

As for the IQP, on-the-job results are harder to assess. The planners of the 1960s hoped that the IQP would better prepare engineering students for participating as informed citizens and professionals in decisions about how technology should be advanced and applied. Whether the IQP has made WPI graduates better able to cope with the Frankenstein complex—technology turning on its creators—remains to be seen. The program is simply too new, and the instruments of assessment too crude, to detect whether conducting an IQP affects beliefs about how technology should be applied.

What WPI has gathered from several surveys is that students feel more confident about their professional abilities after having completed IQPs. Working in teams with partners from different majors, engaging in issues often proposed by off-campus groups, seeking advice from faculty in more than one discipline—all these activities sharpen students' perceptions of the multifaceted nature of work in the professional world. Seeking information from beyond conventional academic sources refines the skills of probing for solutions to problems.

In sum, experience with both the IQP and the MQP programs begins to show engineering and science students that many problems have no simple solutions. Unlike many of the assignments in major fields, a project admits of no single right answer. Solutions—if there are any—are diverse, differently weighted, and skewed by communities of interest. In the MQP, textbook-based problem solving breaks down, and ideal solutions fade in the light of the real world. In the IQP, technical answers interact with social and cultural needs. Students learn to value views and opinions from people outside their own fields, and the complexity of trying to reach resolutions in the real world starts to dawn. As one alumnus said recently about the value of projects, "The MQP got me started in my career, and the IQP changed my life."

William R. Grogan is dean of undergraduate studies at Worcester Polytechnic Institute. He is a professor of electrical engineering.

Lance E. Schachterle is chairman of interdisciplinary affairs and professor of English at Worcester Polytechnic Institute.

Francis C. Lutz is associate dean of undergraduate studies at Worcester Polytechnic Institute. He is a professor of civil engineering.

Successful internship experiences can help students translate experiences in the world of professional work into appropriate academic knowledge and abilities.

The Teachable Moment: The Washington Center Internship Program

Mary Ryan

Approximately one in five students in this country participates in internships (J. Kendall, personal conversation, 1988). Such programs have a long history in the world of education; they also speak to recent calls for more active, involved learning. On many campuses, students seek out and value such off-campus experiences: Alumni of one internship program in Washington, D.C., report that the semester in the capital is "the single most powerful experience" of their undergraduate years (Vick, 1987). Faculty, in contrast, are often skeptical of off-campus experiential learning, asking—and rightly—how such experiences advance the purposes of higher education.

Legitimate questions can be asked, for instance, about the substance of off-campus experiences. What is the relationship between what goes on at the internship site and a knowledge of the liberal arts? In what way is the internship appropriate to the kinds and levels of learning expected in courses in the student's major? How can "busyness" and task completion be distinguished from actual learning? Granted that significant learning may occur, how do we know? Who should certify such learning? Are such off-campus experiences really the best use of educational resources?

P. Hutchings and A. Wutzdorff (eds.). *Knowing and Doing: Learning Through Experience.*
New Directions for Teaching and Learning, no. 35. San Francisco: Jossey-Bass, Fall 1988.

This chapter argues that these questions must and can be addressed, and that internships, properly structured and monitored, can be a powerful tool for learning: "When it is carefully conceived and scrupulously implemented, experiential learning contributes to the highest quality education. The result can be an enhanced capacity on the part of students to develop insights and personal qualities to the fullest extent" (Hook and Fern, 1983). An analysis of the Washington Center internship program suggests that powerful and appropriate learning results when internships give students an experience of intense involvement, coupled with sustained, systematic reflection.

The Washington Center

Founded in 1975 as a nonprofit educational organization, the Washington Center offers college students opportunities in the nation's capital for full-time internships in a broad range of academic disciplines. Affiliated with over six hundred colleges and universities nationwide, the center works in partnership with home institutions and internship sites to extend students' learning.

Each college or university affiliate selects a campus liaison, a person who alerts students to the opportunities for internships in Washington, D.C., and monitors their progress once placed. Liaisons may establish and oversee campus-specific requirements for internship students, and they receive the written reports and evaluations of their interns' on-site work.

Agency sponsors from internship sites work as partners with campus liaisons. The Washington Center currently works with over one thousand sponsors—professionals in public, private, and nonprofit organizations offering internships appropriate to most disciplines. The placement process is carefully supervised to ensure that sponsors provide work that is worthy of credit (defined as 80 percent substantive) and that they monitor their interns' progress through ongoing observation and feedback on performance.

Another set of partners is the Washington Center's program associates. With these staff members, students discuss placement options and decide on sites appropriate to their areas of study and their learning goals. Program associates then guide their students through the entire internship experience, from placement through the final evaluation, providing ongoing support, arranging special activities, and working with campus liaisons, as appropriate.

The students who participate in the Washington Center program come from across the country and represent a broad range of academic disciplines (although, not surprisingly, political interests run especially high). They are generally highly motivated and goal-oriented, very serious about the impact of education on their future. A survey of alumni indicates that before attending the Washington Center, 84 percent had participated in student organizations, 44 percent had held positions related to their career goals (before or during college), and 30 percent had participated in student government (Vick, 1987). Washington Center interns are also risk takers, willing to leave a safe, familiar learning environment and close friends for the unknown and (as they soon discover) demanding world of work in Washington, D.C.

The Teachable Moment

Naturally, the Washington Center has unique features. Like other successful off-campus experiential programs, however, it represents a powerful and extended "teachable moment," when conditions for learning are ripe, and when things come together. As juniors or seniors, students bring to their internships considerable background in their areas of study. They have knowledge and abilities ready to be tested and applied to new contexts; motivation runs high. For them, experiential learning constitutes "the point of integration of theory and practice and of educational and professional experience" (Ferringer and Jacobs, 1984).

Moreover, internships present an alternative way to learn. Experiential learning is more active, concrete, and personal—and considerably less structured—than learning in the classroom. Students must combine the knowledge and skills acquired in the classroom and apply them to professional settings. Particularly powerful learning occurs "outside of the classroom, where problems are real, solutions complex, and individualized challenges possible" (Macala, 1986).

More specifically, internships like those provided by the Washington Center enable students to translate and adapt the academic conventions of, say, writing a term paper or a research report to the real-world demands of drafting a policy study for a congressional subcommittee. Both tasks require hours of research, writing skills, analysis, logic, and the ability to draw conclusions. The policy study, however, allows a student to test and refine classroom theories about, for example, decision making and the mechanisms of social change. Similarly, a placement in the National Gallery of Art both confirms and challenges what the art history major has learned of painting styles and periods.

Finally, an internship promotes a more personal kind of learning than most students experience in the classroom. In their evaluations of the Washington Center program, interns report that some of their most powerful experiences are of personal development. To adapt to and cope with a new living environment, they must become more autonomous. New and different professional responsibilities test their strengths and weaknesses. They question the relevance of their major fields of study and begin to clarify their career goals. They learn how to cope with office politics and to manage complex interpersonal relations. As a result of encountering different ideas and beliefs, they come to understand their own views more clearly.

Observation by the center's staff, agency sponsors, and campus liaisons confirm students' reports, but such changes do not happen automatically or accidentally; living in a different place or doing different things will not in itself ensure learning. As Chickering (1977) points out, "In large measure, the problems of experiential learning are simply those of good teaching. There are complex questions concerning purpose, substance, and quality; concerning students' abilities and differences; concerning the contribution and sequence of various learning activities; concerning evaluation and certification."

At the Washington Center, an internship means close supervision, support, and evaluation. In addition, two primary strategies turn on-site experience into substantive learning: involving students in deliberate overload, and requiring them to engage in sustained, systematic self-reflection on what they know and do.

Learning Overload

Astin's (1984) research shows that learning increases when students are active and engaged. "Quite simply," he explains, "student involvement refers to the amount of physical and psychological energy the student devotes to the academic experience." The extent to which students achieve particular developmental goals is "a direct function of the time and effort they devote to activities designed to produce these gains." At the Washington Center, students experience an extreme form of involvement, a sort of deliberate learning overload.

Living in Washington is in itself stressful. Many students come to the internship from rural areas, with no experience of urban environments. Even those who may have occasionally visited the capital must learn to manage in the city on a daily basis. The first few weeks are a time of overload and intense emotional, intellectual, and physical involvement.

At their sites, students quickly find themselves overloaded with work and related academic requirements. A full-time internship means four and a half days per week at the site; skipping a class is no longer an option. Like everyone else in the office, the student is expected to be present, to contribute, and to be accountable for assigned responsibilities.

Beyond work at the site, the student is required to take an academic seminar equivalent to a three-credit course on campus. Such weekly seminars are generally taught by academics who are also practitioners in their fields. Enrollment is limited to fifteen students per seminar to encourage involvement and discussion. Washington Center internships present no occasions for students to sit back and wait for learning to come to them.

Individual campuses may also impose their own requirements on students. The liaison at Bowling Green State University requires students to write weekly progress reports that reflect critically on their experiences. Many students also write long research papers that integrate their experiences in Washington.

When they are not working or studying or managing the routine tasks of living, students are expected to take advantage of the many learning opportunities available to them in the capital. The Washington Center arranges a variety of activities designed and monitored to maximize student learning. The R. J. Reynolds Presidential Lecture Series on alternate Monday evenings is required of all students. In recent semesters, it has featured such speakers as Amelia Parker, executive director of the Congressional Black Caucus; Senator Strom Thurmond of South Carolina; and Molly Yard, president of the National Organization for Women. Twice each semester, students are invited in groups of thirty to the Capitol Hill Breakfast Series, where they hear from and interact with leaders and policymakers in the Washington area. In addition, program associates may organize tours of the offices of the *Washington Post* or the State Department. Attendance is expected at brown-bag lunches and discussions on topics that may include a current case before the Supreme Court or the workings of the World Bank. In others words, energy and effort are constantly required of interns.

Reflection and Learning

The Washington Center not only requires intense involvement and experience but also structures reflection on that experience into the program. Reflection begins with an extensive application, which students complete before they arrive. Along with recommendations and transcripts, each student must submit a paper on an issue related to his or her area of study and tell how a Washington Center internship will advance that learning. The application thus begins a process of reflection about oneself as a learner, calling on students to articulate their goals and purposes.

Texas Christian University (TCU) goes a step farther. TCU students interested in Washington Center internships must apply almost a year in advance. Those who are selected take a noncredit course with three objectives: counseling and advisement regarding site selection, culminating in the completion of the Washington Center application process; a focus on the liberal arts and social-science skills that may be relevant to professional goals and responsibilities in the internship; and increasing the student's familiarity with the culture, history, and attractions of Washington, D.C. Such preparation focuses students' attention on the how and what, the purposes and contexts, of the internship experience. According to the TCU campus liaison, "Students who participate in this advance experience are better able to take advantage of the opportunities available through the Washington Center program" (E. Alpert, personal communication, 1988). That is, students are better prepared to reflect on the intense involvement they experience as interns.

Of course, all students who join the Washington Center program are expected to engage in ongoing reflection. Having grappled with learning goals in their applications to the program, students must next complete individualized learning contracts. This assignment challenges them to answer in greater detail a variety of questions about their learning: What, specifically, do you plan to learn as a result of your internship? What new knowledge and skills do you hope to acquire? How do you expect to grow personally and professionally as a result of this experience? Program associates review learning contracts and, if necessary, guide students toward more appropriate, realistic, and assessable goals.

Once they begin work at their internship sites, students attend weekly small-group discussions facilitated by program associates. Once again, the focus is on reflection. Talking about their own experiences, and hearing about those of other students at related sites, students are able to distance themselves from the daily routine of tasks and activities. They begin to translate what they are doing into more general knowledge and abilities. A particularly potent strategy has been to have students visit one another's sites and meet with different agency supervisors. This exchange broadens their views of the professional world and provides a framework for reflecting on their own work. One organizing principle of all such reflection is a repeated question: What have you learned, and how have you changed?

The first written evaluation of student learning occurs early in the semester and becomes a benchmark for growth, learning, and change in later discussions and evaluations. Program associates visit students at their internship sites and complete internship formulations, which are a first "snapshot" of the intern functioning in a professional setting. Such visits reinforce students' sense of accountability, not only to agency supervisors and campus liaisons but also to program associates, whose evaluations depend not only on what students are doing but also on what they are learning.

Individual, campus-specific assignments can also promote reflection. Bowling Green State University requires interns to submit weekly progress reports, in which they reflect critically about their experiences and on how what they are doing relates to classroom learning. Questions include the following: What types of experiences have you had? Does what you see fit with what you learned in class? What have you learned about the working of an office or system? What have you learned about our nation's capital and our political system? What have you learned about yourself? Have you changed any of the ways you respond to things? Has anything made you stop and think about your career plans? How have your feelings changed about your work, yourself, and your career?

Not all students are required by campus liaisons to keep logs, but all complete reflective written assignments as part of the requirements of the internship. The midterm evaluation, for instance, is completed by both the student and the agency sponsor, with both focusing on the learning engendered by the internship. The student must address the relationship between on-site projects and activities and the goals and objectives specified in the learning contract. Agency sponsors evaluate transferable skills, such as writing and speaking, and discuss students' creativity and initiative.

The final evaluation builds on the midterm. First, students review their learning goals and assess, against those goals, what they have learned and how; second, they deal with the strengths and the weaknesses of their performance. Agency sponsors do the same. Again, the focal questions are not on what was done but on what the student has learned from that doing. How has she or he performed, and what changes have resulted?

At the end of the semester, the student, the agency sponsor, and the program associate meet for a final summary of the internship. The agency sponsor recommends a grade. Next, the program associate, with an eye toward both on-site internship activities and other program requirements, writes a narrative evaluation, focusing on the student's learning and development. The program associate recommends a final grade to the campus liaison. This grade is usually accepted.

Outcomes and Impacts

In 1987, the Washington Center commissioned a survey of its alumni to assess their perceptions of the internship experience. (A survey instrument from Alverno College was adapted for this purpose.) Some significant findings emerged (Vick, 1987).

First, alumni reported that the internships were particularly helpful for identifying areas where additional learning was needed. Indeed, 67 percent said they had recognized skill deficiencies during their internships. Most frequently cited as areas of deficiency were writing skills, oral communication, and self-confidence. More important, students reported that they worked to improve in these areas, taking additional courses after returning to campus, strengthening themselves in graduate school, and participating in other internships.

A significant number of alumni reported that their internships resulted in clarification of career goals. Asked about the relationship between their internships and their first jobs, 61 percent reported that the internships provided "good to excellent preparation"; 65 percent reported that the internships provided "good to excellent potential for advancement" in their first jobs. One alumnus said, "Everything came directly into play as soon as I began my job. No entry-level position could be as fulfilling as my internship, and I knew I was able to handle more. I just had to prove it to my supervisors" (Vick, 1987).

In addition to their observations about goals related to future work, many Washington Center alumni reported indirect or unanticipated effects: 90 percent indicated that the program had increased their awareness of world issues and social problems. One commented, "The Washington Center opened my eyes to how our political system revolves. It helped to nurture and develop my political philosophy and my later interest in public affairs" (Vick, 1987).

Besides using the 1987 alumni survey, the Washington Center has regularly asked students to evaluate their internship experiences and their effects. Students consistently report that they have grown dramatically in their ability to cope with change and to tolerate different attitudes and expectations. They report that they learn to manage their time, improve their organizational skills, and practice different writing styles. They learn, in some cases for the first time, how to do research, and why it matters. They report that their self-confidence has improved, and that they have come to see themselves as professionals who have knowledge and skills to contribute to society.

Most students report that they have improved their writing, critical thinking, and decision making, and that real-world tasks and consequences propel such improvement. Such experiences differ, they say, from selecting a topic for a research paper, doing library research, and turning in a final product. They say they work harder because assignments are real, and they feel that they are contributing to a significant, known outcome.

The majority of students reports having "miraculously changed" during the internship. Needless to say, Washington Center educators have a different view, in which growth and development can be attributed to how the program is structured and monitored. An effective internship includes intense involvement, ongoing reflection, support, evaluation, and frequent feedback. Partners in the learning process must understand their own roles. Agency sponsors must view themselves as educators; program associates and faculty liaisons must help students reflect on what they are learning and on how their experiences relate to academic studies. The next step will be to institute a more systematic assessment of how internships contribute to learning, so that experiential programs like the Washington Center can be made even more powerful.

References

Astin, A. W. "Student Involvement: A Developmental Theory of Higher Education." *Journal of College Student Personnel*, 1984, *24* (4), 297–308.

Chickering, A. W. *Experience and Learning: An Introduction to Experiential Learning.* New Rochelle, N.Y.: Change Magazine Press, 1977.

Ferringer, F. R., and Jacobs, E. *A Three Parameter Model for Planning, Monitoring, and Evaluating Human Services Field Experience.* Omaha, Nebr.: EDIC Associates, 1984.

Hook, W., and Fern, S. P. "Internship in Social Science: An Historical Perspective and Suggestions for the Future." *Innovative Higher Education*, 1983, *8* (1), 431.

Macala, J. C. "Sponsored Experiential Program—Learning by Doing in the Workplace." In L. H. Lewis (ed.), *Experiential and Simulation Techniques for Teaching Adults.* New Directions for Continuing Education, no. 30. San Francisco: Jossey-Bass, 1986.

Vick, D. S. Alumni survey compiled for the Washington Center. Washington, D.C.: The Washington Center, 1987.

Mary Ryan is vice-president for academic affairs at the Washington Center.

Through self-assessment, students take increasing responsibility
for their own learning and move toward more integrated,
complex forms of knowledge and ability.

Self-Assessment: Essential Skills for Adult Learners

David O. Justice, Catherine Marienau

Adults return to school for a multitude of reasons. They wish to resume interrupted education. They need credentials to qualify for new jobs or promotions. There are skills, perspectives, or knowledge they want to acquire to live more fully. They often wish to fulfill commitments they have made to themselves and others.

As adults, they come to learning with a variety of life skills, experience, and knowledge. Some of these skills and knowledge they are aware of and proudly display; others they may practice without being fully conscious of what they are doing or how their knowledge is used, and they rarely relate what they know to college learning.

Most postsecondary programs for adults respond to the diversity of adult learners by providing a relatively wide range of courses and classes. Most commonly, programs for adult learners are delivered at times and in locations more convenient than ever before. Many programs offer individualized counseling and academic advising. With increasing frequency, colleges and universities also offer some form of assessment of adults' skills and knowledge for the purposes of advanced placement and credit.

Self-assessment offers an important element for programs seeking to

P. Hutchings and A. Wutzdorff (eds.). *Knowing and Doing: Learning Through Experience.*
New Directions for Teaching and Learning, no. 35. San Francisco: Jossey-Bass, Fall 1988.

serve adult learners. By learning to systematically engage in self-assessment, adult learners can ascertain and clarify their needs and motivations for learning, identify learning goals, and measure the achievement of their learning. Self-assessment places the locus of control within the learner and draws on the best source of information about the characteristics of the learner. It directly enlists the student's motivation for learning and relates the outcomes of the learning enterprise to the initial reasons for beginning it. The skills of self-assessment can become an integral component of the learning outcomes of many adult programs.

The School for New Learning

The power of self-assessment is a key principle of the School for New Learning (SNL), an alternative degree program for adult learners and one of the six colleges of DePaul University. SNL began with the assumption that students, and adult learners in particular, come to school with significant college-level learning that may or may not be certified by accredited institutions of higher education. The idea that colleges could evaluate such learning at all was, and in some quarters still is, controversial. Thus, much of the early work on assessment of knowledge, skills, and abilities focused on gaining external validation: How could the knowledge that students had gained from their work or avocational pursuits be reasonably determined, and what would be its academic worth? The means of assessment usually focused on faculty-based evaluations of performance, most often in written form.

As the SNL curriculum developed and the emphasis on individualized learning grew, the importance of assessment as a part of the learner's capability and responsibility became apparent. Educated adults are expected to make responsible decisions, solve problems, and engage in self-managed learning. They develop and exercise the skills of goal setting, problem framing and solving, planning, diagnosis, critical thinking, and analysis. In their roles as productive and responsible citizens, they must regularly analyze and evaluate people, products, and programs from all sectors of contemporary life. The skills of self-assessment, as well as the habit of mind that turns to self-assessment at the appropriate time, are essential parts of the repertoire of educated men and women. Thus, for SNL, developing our students' skills of self-assessment has become an integral part of the curriculum.

SNL: An Overview

Serving one thousand students annually, the School for New Learning offers B.A. and M.A. programs. Both are structured around outcome criteria—explicit statements of the knowledge and ability expected of successful degree candidates. Focusing on the outcomes of learning has several advantages for SNL's adult learners. It allows maximum flexibility in the design of individual programs. It sets a framework for integrating and assessing knowledge and abilities gained outside of college. Most important, by focusing students' attention on what they need to achieve and at what level of expertise, outcome criteria foster the habit of self-assessment.

Stimulating, modeling, and reinforcing self-assessment is a central thrust of both the B.A. and M.A. core curricula. Students begin with a preadmission workshop, in which they reflect on themselves as learners. At this initial stage, self-assessment activities are presented in a structured but open-ended manner. Inventories of skills, areas of knowledge or expertise, and work experiences are discussed. A learning-style inventory is administered to help the adult learner appreciate her own style of learning and become aware of the diversity of styles among her peers. In some workshops, candidates for admission may also take a personality inventory, which is used to show learners relevant characteristics of learning and provide them with a language for discussing their similarities and differences.

The second component of the core curriculum is a course to design a learning plan. In this course, learners focus on assessing what they know and how to document it, what they need to learn to achieve their own goals and the requirements of the program, and how they will learn it. In the process of designing a plan, the learner confronts the issue of standards: What are the internal and often implicit standards of one's own life and work, and what are the standards of the workplace or the university? How can these be brought into congruence?

The third component of the core curriculum requires that each student's plan be developed with and supported by a committee, which consists of a faculty member, a professional from the student's chosen field, and often a peer. The committee provides a forum in which the student examines her plans in relationship to the requirements of the external world in which she functions.

A course in research and inquiry is the fourth component of the SNL core curriculum. This course helps the learner use formal and informal methods to identify and clarify issues for investigation and problem solving. Grounded in the work and life experiences of the learner, the inquiry course focuses on problem-framing techniques, the use of resources, and the role of research in decision making.

The fifth component of the core curriculum deals with assessment itself. Students are given the opportunity to examine what has been happening in their programs. What knowledge, skills, and abilities have they used in their lives outside of school, and how? Which learning activities have worked for them, and why? They are encouraged to use the language of learning styles, as well as the standards and criteria of the program, in their descriptions.

Making use of this assessment, the learner is asked to design and execute an independent learning project, drawing on the formal learning skills gained through the previous work in SNL and on her knowledge of herself. Each independent learning project is discussed with and approved by the committee. The independent project provides the learner with less formal structure and more challenge, as she is asked to exercise both formal knowledge of an area or discipline and knowledge of herself. In the independent project, the adult student is asked to draw on her work or life experiences, as well as on the academic knowledge gained from school.

The seventh component of the core curriculum is the culminating colloquium. This final activity asks the learner to draw together the experiences of her program of study at the school and to evaluate them in terms of her own goals and objectives, the goals of the school, and the standards and criteria of the work world as she has come to know it. In the colloquium the learner is asked to exercise the skills of self-assessment in the form of a reflective integration of what has gone on before.

The Practice of Self-Assessment

SNL uses four strategies to develop self-assessment skills in students: storytelling, development of standards, dialogue, and inquiry.

Storytelling. SNL students begin work on self-assessment through storytelling. In preadmission workshops, they are asked to write educational autobiographies, or descriptions of their practice of their professions. In their own terms, they describe the significant learning events in their personal and professional lives.

In this way, candidates begin to look at themselves as individual learners with identifiable characteristics and ways of approaching problems and conceiving of solutions. They begin to value themselves as learners and to be able to describe themselves with clarity and precision. In small-group exercises, students share their new understanding of themselves and compare their perceptions with those of their fellow learners. Listening to one another's stories helps them see their own characteristics more clearly. The habit of reflecting on knowledge, insights, and understanding about oneself has begun.

Self-assessment, then, begins with telling one's own story and finding a language for self-description. Often, students, and adult learners in particular, are expected to come to college already knowing themselves. The curriculum begins either with a prescription for what one must learn or with a variety of choices from which one is expected to choose.

In contrast, asking students to tell their own stories focuses learning on the learner. It reinforces the legitimacy of the self and helps create a coherent structure on which to build new learning. As the adult student understands herself as a learner, she becomes better equiped to identify, recognize, and create meaningful constructs in her environment that are congruent with herself. Telling her own story also places her at the center of the action.

The language of inventories and assessment instruments can help people think about themselves and communicate with others with greater precision, but it is not a sufficient base on which to build the skills and habits of self-assessment. Learners need to find their own voices to describe themselves and their competence. The next task, then, is for students to learn to recognize, understand, and finally create standards for self-assessment.

Development of Standards. The second step in developing skill in self-assessment comes when students begin to generate their own criteria for assessment. In the School for New Learning, this step is begun in the core curriculum course on designing a learning plan, where students examine the categories around which their own learning will be structured and then prepare statements that describe the intended outcomes of their learning.

Students first come to an understanding of the language of learning outcomes and then examine the implications of the statements. Key to this experience is the manner in which the learner relates new categories and definitions to her own ways of thinking about what she knows and can do. Initially, the reaction is often despair: "I don't possess any competence at all." As learners become more aware of the content of learning and of the performance implications of competence, they gain more confidence: "I can do that. I've done that in my company for the past three years." By linking their accomplishments with some of the statements of learning outcomes, learners gain a new understanding of the statements of competence and of the relation between conceptual knowledge and its application to life and work settings. The confidence they gain in interpreting the meanings of these outcomes helps them to move on to more difficult levels and to begin to articulate some of their own knowledge and skills in terms of learning outcomes.

Moreover, the framework provided by outcome criteria helps students relate what they know to what they can do. In an SNL seminar, a student described the task of editing a science text for fifth graders in terms of a model of interpersonal communications. The standards of the school, outcome statements, serve as a model or template for students to use as they develop their own standards. By judging herself first against the standards of the school and then against the standards she has developed, the learner moves closer to self-assessment.

Initially, criteria provided by the school are more or less passively accepted. From time to time, the assertive learner will challenge a definition or an approach, but the common assumption is that the school has its standards and that students are here to achieve them. Nevertheless, self-assessment against an external standard falls short of the learning potential of self-assessment. By learning how categories are fashioned, and then by defining their own categories, students learn to shape criteria. A competence statement written by the college can be a model for how to express a valued attribute. As students complete the course on the design of a learning plan, they gain the tools to define categories for assessing both prior and future learning.

Dialogue. Talking with others—mentors, advisers, teachers or peers— is a powerful way for the learner to monitor how clearly she is expressing her own purposes or how well she is meeting certain standards of her educational program. In dialogue with others, the learner is encouraged to reflect critically on her thinking and her actions. A trusting relationship with others helps minimize the risks of looking critically at herself and of exploring new ideas and ways of thinking. Furthermore, the learner is encouraged to experiment with new ways of learning that she might not try otherwise.

Most learners are apprehensive at the outset of their programs about their ability to manage the learning process and achieve acceptable outcomes. The SNL program provides a formal system of support for the learner, the academic committee, which helps her monitor and evaluate her progress toward degree goals.

Looking back on her educational experience at the point of graduation, an undergraduate said, "My committee gave me lots of feedback on my work and my overall progress. My mentor especially encouraged me to assess my own strengths and, as a result, I became bolder and more risk-taking in my learning." The committee she referred to is a team composed of herself, a faculty mentor, and an outside practitioner in her area of concentration. They have worked together since the earliest phase of her development of a learning plan. Several strategies characterize that work and suggest the power of dialogue to help develop self-assessment skills.

First, the academic committee must listen to the learner's stories. She comes to the committee with her autobiography. This reflective overview has been initiated in the preadmission phase and refined in the program-planning phase. In the committee, the learner shifts her story from a review of the past to a projection of the future—that is, to her goals and strategies for achieving them.

Second, during the process of implementing these strategies, the committee must offer a balance of support and challenge. Supportive dialogue affirms the learner's existing ways of judging her experience. Her willingness to engage in self-assessment is enhanced by her knowledge that she is accepted as she sees herself. Challenging dialogue stimulates the learner to refine and add to her skills of applying criteria to her own behaviors and achievements. That may mean getting her to question her inner structures of meaning by giving direct criticism or by creating situations that test her assumptions. Two cases illustrate how dialogue can engage learners in self-assessment with fruitful results. In the first case, an undergraduate learner gains perspective on achieving a career goal that until now has seemed beyond reach. In the second case, a learner in the graduate program acquires skills that help her make stronger connections between practice and theory in her professional setting.

Toni, an undergraduate, dreams of having a career in psychology, perhaps as a therapist in private practice or as an organizational development specialist in a corporate setting. Her dilemma, as she calls it, is that she is forty years old, has completed less than one year of college, and combines homemaking responsibilities with school and full-time work as a secretary.

Toni expresses several frustrations to her committee. She does not know which branch of psychology to choose as her focus. She faces many years of formal study and training. She has "lots of learning experience, but none that count for anything" toward psychology.

Toni's committee takes her stated goal seriously and acknowledges that she does indeed have a long road ahead. The committee recognizes that Toni's anxious preoccupation with achieving that distant goal is interfering with her setting specific, realistic goals and enjoying successes along the way.

The committee helps Toni direct her attention toward setting short-term goals, beginning with identifying what she already knows that is relevant to psychology. For the first time, the committee hears about the couples-communication groups that she and her husband colead for the church, about the church-based nursery school she initiated and staffed for several years, and about the self-directed reading she has done in the literature of child and adult development. Thus, from these past experiences, the committee helps Toni identify significant learning that gives her a foundation for proceeding in psychology.

The committee also advises Toni to monitor how her interests develop in various aspects of psychology over the next year. She agrees to take a series of recommended self-report inventories that may provide additional information about her work interests and aptitudes.

Toni's committee listens and asks questions to find out about her world and her view of it. The members support her long-range goals by helping her recognize relevant experience and set more specific goals. The committee challenges her to use her time not only to learn new subject matter but also to develop a sense of herself as a professional.

The committee has created an environment in which Toni is able to carry on a reflective dialogue about who she is and who she is becoming. She also gains a more positive and realistic view of the standards of the profession she pursues and of what she can accomplish.

The case of Janet, a seasoned professional in the graduate program, illustrates how the committee teaches a strategy for self-assessment that helps the learner acknowledge and meet standards that extend beyond her specific setting. The graduate program expects learners to transform appropriate work-based projects into academic learning. Janet consistently receives high praise from her superiors and colleagues for her performance as manager of the development office for a nonprofit agency. Nevertheless, she has difficulty communicating the base of knowledge behind her actions and evaluating her work. Janet wants her committee to accept her successful efforts to increase the agency's external funding base as evidence that she knows theories of nonprofit management. The committee, however, expects Janet to articulate her knowledge and, equally important, to develop appropriate criteria for judging her own work.

The committee gives Janet a task to help her develop criteria and apply them to herself. She is to select a management problem from her workplace and, in writing, address these questions: What is the management problem, and what are its various dimensions? How is this management problem similar to and different from other management problems I have solved successfully? What concepts and principles will guide my approach to this problem? What criteria will I have met when the problem is resolved successfully? With each iteration, Janet becomes more articulate and concise in her responses and more reflective about the criteria that are emerging. As Janet tries to decipher the meaning of the committee's challenge, she is assessing her own purposes and actions.

For both Janet and Toni, the academic committee uses the strategies of good dialogue—listening, supporting, challenging—to foster better skills of self-assessment. Daloz (1986, p. 225) calls this process "developmental dialogue," because it helps the learner express her goals as well as her problems, monitor her progress, and interpret what she is accomplishing in light of her own and external standards. Toni is learning to monitor her evolving career goals and to judge her learning in light of those goals. Janet is gaining appreciation for, and some skill in, judging her own performance against appropriate standards. Both learners become able to reflect on their behavior and set new courses of action for more productive learning.

Inquiry. Janet's case also recalls the importance of the learner's being able to set criteria for judging her own performance. One essential aspect is the ability to acquire new knowledge through appropriate inquiry. The process of investigating new subject areas gives the learner practice in applying internal standards for her own performance and formulating criteria for the processes by which she acquires new knowledge.

At SNL, undergraduate and graduate learners are instructed in the methods of research and inquiry that are important building blocks for learners. Undergraduates in particular cite the course in research and inquiry as a highlight of their educational experience. As one learner says, "It gives me tools for finding out and confidence for doing it." For practitioner/graduate students, who are particularly in need of applied research methods, the course provides useful problem-solving tools for learning and action in their places of work.

Acquiring tools of inquiry helps put individuals in control of their own learning. Confidence in knowing how to find out contributes to the learner's willingness and ability to engage in self-assessment of how well she is framing problems, finding and using resources, and using results in decision making.

The courses in research and inquiry, at both the undergraduate and graduate levels, employ a discovery approach, which proceeds from the learner's own questions to explorations that help elaborate and refine those questions, the actual design of a research effort, and articulation of criteria for the soundness of the inquiry process. As the first step, the learner selects her own topic of inquiry, typically one having personal or professional relevance. For example, a learner has been primary caretaker for three years for a family member who suffers from Alzheimer's disease. She is free to investigate this topic if she frames it from the perspective of her selected outcome area, science and health. She chooses to focus her inquiry on how Alzheimer's disease affects the physiology of the brain.

The second step in the inquiry process gives the learner room to explore and experience her topic. One approach is to explore secondary sources (for example, through library research) in search of primary issues and a focus for the topic. As a more experiential approach, the learner frames a problem that stems directly from her own experience. For the student investigating Alzheimer's disease, for instance, resources are dictated by the kinds of questions she asks from her firsthand experience with an individual whose brain is dysfunctional.

In the third step, the learner proposes a design for finding out about the topic. The proposed design includes the framing of the problem, the resources and methods to be used, and the expected outcomes or results. The design also should reflect the inclusion of internal and external criteria. For example, in the graduate program, the learner must indicate how her proposed project will do at least two of the following things: show a grasp of current knowledge or practice in a field, gather original information or data, prove or disprove a hypothesis, apply theory to practice, develop theory out of practice, and interpret original information or data. These criteria help the learner meet standards of graduate-level learning. She must be able to determine the appropriate fit between her inquiry project and these external criteria.

The fourth step further develops the learner's emerging sense of criteria for what constitutes sound inquiry. With the help of her instructor and peers, she must try to articulate criteria for doing adequate inquiry. The criteria must emerge from her reflection on her own experience. To draw on an earlier example, let us say that the learner elects to formulate her own hypothesis about brain dysfunction and bases it on careful observations of the family member stricken with Alzheimer's. She also chooses to substantiate the soundness of her ideas with documentation from medical research. During her inquiry, she must reflect on the strengths and limitations of her approach and her findings.

The learner also benefits from the experiences of her classmates, who are engaged in the same process. Individually and collectively, learners gain skills in applying external rules of inquiry. Further, they develop a more sophisticated set of internal criteria for judging their own and others' performance. They expand their repertoire of self-assessment skills by being able to apply their reflective and evaluative abilities to new areas of knowledge.

Reflection in Action

Storytelling, development of standards, dialogue, and inquiry—these dimensions of self-assessment, woven together, are crucial to the integration of knowing and doing. Moreover, a key to such integration lies in self-assessment, which, to borrow Schön's (1983) term, involves a reflection in action. Basically, the process flows out of an individual's tacit knowledge, the confronting of something in the environment that does not quite fit, which leads to "reflection within an action-present" and sometimes results in the person's being able to "restructure strategies of action, understandings of phenomena, or ways of framing problems" (Schön, 1987, p. 28). For adult students, who are adapting their learning to a variety of modes and contexts, this sophisticated form of self-assessment seems imperative for effective learning.

In the SNL core curriculum, the learner practices her ability to reflect in action through independent learning projects. She must create her own categories for learning, which, in the SNL context, means writing her own statements of specific learning outcomes. She must carry out and monitor the activity, adjusting her approach whenever new information is encountered. She must devise the criteria by which an expert will evaluate the outcomes, and she must evaluate her performance as a learner. The following two independent learning efforts illustrate the widening range of the criteria and contexts in which SNL learners engage in self-assessment.

The first illustration is from the undergraduate program, in which the learner is required to design and carry out an independent project in an area that is new or unfamiliar in some significant way. Given that this project is undertaken toward the end of her program, SNL expects her to have developed flexibility in her ability successfully to manage a new learning effort.

Toby selected an independent project that addressed several purposes. She admired people who had a "passion" for their hobbies and, having dabbled in several hobbies, with unsatisfying results, wanted to find a hobby that engaged her interest and creativity. Further, Toby had recently purchased a two-story house in need of extensive rehabilitation, and she knew nothing about this kind of work.

She designed a project consisting of three related activities: taking a community-based course in residential rehabilitation, developing a master plan for rehabilitation of her house, and monitoring her learning process and reflecting on her performance. Toby generally preferred learning activities that were structured by the instructor and that had clearly delineated steps leading to known outcomes. Her project promised new learning with respect to the subject area, the learning process, and the learning methods (inspecting houses in various states of repair, reading about principles and methods of house construction, creating blueprints for her own house, and testing her blueprints against expert opinion).

As part of the outcome statements that would guide her work and its evaluation, Toby used such phrases as "can devise a plan for rehabilitation of residential property, using project-management techniques" and "understands the principles of design and construction management necessary to complete residential housing projects."

The final excerpts from Toby's project log tell an important story about her learning experience and her capacity for self-assessment: "I have more confidence in myself. I came to realize that when I undertake something new, I tend to worry more about my ability to perform the task at hand than to concentrate on enjoying the process of learning something different. I believe this realization came about because I was forced to focus on the learning process (by maintaining a logbook) and not on the master plan. I became involved in the process. As a result, I realized the enjoyment of working through something new. I am positive that I will approach my next learning experience, whether formal or informal, with a slightly different attitude. I'm going to try to leave myself open for experimenting and not concern myself so much with whether I can do something or not."

Toby, of course, is not suggesting that she will abandon high standards for her own products; indeed, her final product was an excellent demonstration of her competence. Rather, she is talking about learning, first, to learn more effectively in a wider variety of situations and, second, to have confidence in applying the learning skills she has acquired. Further, she is developing the capacity for reflection in action, which lets her know when she is being open or closed to new experiences and when she is concentrating too heavily on achieving a product and neglecting performance.

The second illustration is from the graduate program, which gives learners the opportunity to monitor the development of their abilities in liberal learning (problem framing and solving, verbal communication, interpersonal skills, values in decision making, and moral reasoning) as they pursue independent learning activities in their professional settings. At approximately three-month intervals during the first year of the program, learners meet with program faculty to share assessments of their performance. They draw on entries in their activity journals, in which they have recorded their behavior during specific events that have happened in their workplaces.

This approach to self-assessment encourages learners both to reflect in action and to reflect on their behavior after an event. The approach also gives learners time to recognize significant areas of growth and improvement in performance. For example, a marketing specialist says she is becoming better at conceptualizing problems and more aware of the action process. The head of a health-care economics research department says that he has become more conscious of his decision-making process and how he frames problems, and he now conducts finer analyses of problems. A policeman notes that he is now taking a proactive approach to problem solving, learning to look at problems from all key perspectives.

A candidate for graduation, reflecting on her learning experiences, has been made, she says, "keenly and continuously aware of the impact of the learning process on my professional life." She reports that applying the self-assessment process has helped her evaluate and improve her professional performance. She notes significant improvements—for example, in her ability to manage employees and market the services of her firm. She has also developed more sophisticated understandings of leadership and has assumed greater leadership responsibilities in other arenas of her profession.

Thus, independent learning engages learners in assessing not only what they have learned, but also the process by which that learning has occurred, as well as their management of it. Having gained skills in assessing the quality of their own performance, learners are able to focus on transferring their special skills and abilities to a variety of academic and professional contexts.

Reflective Integration

At the conclusion of the SNL programs, learners engage in an intensive examination of their learning and of the work they have produced as part of their learning programs. In the concluding colloquium, students practice their skills of self-assessment as they retrace their steps, from entry through completion and realization of their learning plans.

They engage again in the process of telling their own stories, this time from the perspective of the end of one journey and the beginning of another. Learners present short oral descriptions of their final projects. In small groups, learners discuss their own work and place it in the context of the work of other group members. The opportunity to see the overall productivity, range, and depth of work done by oneself and others reinforces the sense of oneself as an individual learner with a defined place in the community of learners.

These formal and informal presentations offer opportunities to exchange insights and compare common experiences in the process of learning. As they critique, discuss, and elaborate on the themes and issues raised by the reports, learners draw on the language and habits of the self-assessment skills they have gained in the core curriculum. Often, discussions in the concluding colloquium reflect the dialogues of the committee meetings, but the discussions go well beyond the practices of the classroom. They engender thoughtful assessments of the subjects treated in the final projects: "Why is a survey of data-management professionals the best source of determining the future development of computer use by midlevel management?" "How do training programs affect the profitability of small businesses?"

Learners also evaluate the total SNL program during the concluding colloquium. Both individually and as a group, the learners assess the relevance, effectiveness, and personal benefits of each course in the core curriculum and of the courses taken toward completion of their learning plans. While their perspectives provide important feedback to the program faculty and staff, the act of looking back is also an important exercise in completing the dialogue between the individual standards and those of the group. Individuals often cite different courses as unusually effective or meaningful. Discussion in the colloquium uncovers how the skills of self-assessment have been used effectively to measure internal standards against those of the school and those of colleagues.

In the capacity for self-assessment, as it is developed at SNL, are contained the skills, motivation, and capacity for reflection associated with truly educated people, the capacity to see things clearly and in their own terms. Self-assessment implies and entails the analytical tools to take an idea apart and examine its components; the ability to marshall one's mind and one's commitment behind an idea, problem, issue, or cause; and the perspective from which to view each problem or issue in a larger context. Because these are essential goals for adult learning, self-assessment has become an intrinsic part of the curriculum at the School for New Learning.

References

Daloz, L. A. *Effective Teaching and Mentoring: Realizing the Transformational Power of Adult Learning Experiences.* San Francisco: Jossey-Bass, 1986.

Schön, D. A. *The Reflective Practitioner.* New York: Basic Books, 1983.

Schön, D. A. *Educating the Reflective Practitioner: Toward a New Design for Teaching and Learning in the Professions.* San Francisco: Jossey-Bass, 1987.

David O. Justice is dean of DePaul University's School for New Learning (SNL). He was senior program officer at FIPSE and serves on the board of trustees of CAEL.

Catherine Marienau is associate professor and director of the SNL Master's Program. She has held administrative, teaching, and advising positions in individualized programs for adults since 1970.

Goal setting, self-reflection, and other strategies help teach students how to learn from their own experiences on and off campus.

An Integrating Seminar: Bringing Knowledge and Experience Together

Allen Wutzdorff, Pat Hutchings

Knowledge and experience can be powerful partners in advancing stu-*o* dents' learning when systematically structured into a curriculum. Knowledge is made deeper when tested by experience. This knowledge in turn serves as a more focused lens for extracting meaning from new experiences. This chapter offers specific strategies for bringing knowing and doing together in the context of a seminar for students who are doing part-time internships along with their other courses. The chapter concludes with a closer look at two students as they write and reflect about their own learning during their internships. The learning derived from these experiences is related to more than the internships themselves; it builds upon strategies to integrate knowing and doing throughout the curriculum.

At this point, some background information on Alverno College will be helpful (see also Chapter One of this volume). Alverno is a liberal arts college with an ability-based curriculum. As students advance through courses, they are required to demonstrate the achievement of eight broad abilities, including communication, problem solving, and social interaction. These are interwoven into courses so that students have the oppor-

P. Hutchings and A. Wutzdorff (eds.). *Knowing and Doing: Learning Through Experience.*
New Directions for Teaching and Learning, no. 35. San Francisco: Jossey-Bass, Fall 1988.

tunity to develop their abilities in the context of an ever-expanding knowledge base. Off-Campus Experiential Learning (OCEL) is a significant component of the curriculum, and all liberal arts students are required to have at least one OCEL experience before graduating.

In the junior year, students meet with their advisers and register for OCEL (a second OCEL is often taken in the senior year). OCEL itself is an experience of eight to ten hours per week, taken along with whatever other courses are in the student's sequence. At the same time, the student registers for an interdisciplinary seminar of all liberal arts students enrolled in OCEL that semester. The seminar is taught by two instructors, usually from the arts and humanities and the behavioral sciences, and it meets for one hour per week. This schedule arose from practical considerations, but it is consistent with the purpose of OCEL: to provide students with the opportunity to learn independently and free them from the constraints of more typical course requirements. The instructors, too, step away from their customary instructional roles and serve more as coaches, guides, or in some cases, mentors.

The seminar is well suited to the integration of knowing and doing. It is distanced, both physically and temporally, from students' off-campus sites, and because it is interdisciplinary, it encourages students to view abstractly the transferable aspects of what and how they are doing at their sites.

Working in this seminar, we have developed three strategies that promote the integration of knowing and doing: goal setting, reading the environment, and reflection. In many ways, the primary goal of the seminar is to get students to reflect—to connect their experiences and probe them for levels of meaning that may not be immediately apparent, to see the relationship between OCEL and their overall learning. Our experience has taught us that students do not always reflect on their own, perhaps especially when they are in an "action" mode. New activities, a new setting, being away from campus—all these factors can create the illusion that much learning is going on. Students are no doubt learning from all this experience, but without specific strategies, we miss an opportunity to make stronger connections with students' overall academic programs.

Goal Setting

One of the objectives listed in the syllabus for the seminar is learning to set goals (personal, professional, and academic) that will organize and direct activity at the internship site. The key word here is *learning*. Our own experience with the seminar has taught us that goal setting can function as a mechanism for pulling together new and often diverse experiences and integrating those experiences with knowledge and skills already acquired. Goals work best if they are developed as a process whereby students shape and refine them in relation to a realistic sense of what will be possible and desirable at a given site. This process begins in the semester before the OCEL experience, when students are meeting with their advisers. They write out general goals they would like to achieve and list them on a form, which advisers review. Initial goals may often be vague and unrealistic (too restrictive or too grandiose).

Once the OCEL experiences begin, students specify more detailed goals and spend time in the seminar delineating how they plan to achieve them. Around the fourth week, when their site supervisors are attending an on-campus workshop, students meet with them and commit themselves to goals agreed to by both parties. These goals are then used to evaluate students' performance at the internship sites. The process continues as students begin to keep logs, where each week they are asked to formulate subgoals for the following week that will advance them toward their overall goals.

Several characteristics of this process allow goals to organize and direct students' learning. First, students formulate and revise their goals from their actual experiences at the sites. Second, the goals are clearly understood by students, supervisors, and the seminar instructors. Third, students are held accountable for the achievement of their goals. While students usually like their OCEL experiences and the level of involvement entailed, they can become so involved in the doing that they fail to reflect on the meaning of their activities. Engaging students in taking ownership of their own goals, rather than having them go through goal setting as a one-time-only exercise, becomes an important factor in students' ability to integrate their work into broader learning frameworks.

Reading the Environment

The term *reading the environment* has come, in our seminar, to stand for a number of related skills, including understanding the purpose of the site, how it is organized to achieve that purpose, its relation to the environment. Whom does it serve? What institutions does it intersect with? Assignments require students to articulate their own roles at their sites and to note any changes that occur over time in their roles or their perceptions of their roles in relation to others at the setting.

In the seminar, faculty initially help students think about what they see and hear around them: to be good observers. It is interesting to us as faculty, and to other students, to observe how a student majoring in art might focus on the physical layout and esthetic appeal of the setting, while a management major turns to concerns of personnel, and a sociology student to organizational structure. It can be helpful to approach this question in untraditional ways. Rather than asking for an analytical essay, for instance, we have asked students to bring something from their sites that they see as a key or clue to the settings as a whole. At another point, students create metaphors that describe their own places and roles at their sites. In this focus on observation, on reading the environment, the student must step back from her involvement at the site. She must distance herself from her own experience in order to see the situation and herself within it. Moreover, in attempting to articulate what she observes for an interdisciplinary group, she must begin translating discrete and particular features into more transferable, abstract learning—for instance, generalizations about organizational structure, or hypotheses about cooperation versus competition in work-related interactions.

Reflecting

A major goal of the OCEL seminar is to develop students' ability to reflect on work at the sites in order to monitor and shape the learning it yields. All activities and assessments are directed toward this end. To put it somewhat differently, although we are concerned with what the student does at the site and how well she does it, we are more concerned with what she learns from what she does. Indeed, the college's entire program is grounded in the distinction between doing for the sake of doing and doing that is translated, through analysis and reflection, into learning that can be abstracted and transferred to new situations. The issue is not whether a management student is able to complete a balance sheet to the satisfaction of her mentor (although this is important), but whether she is able to articulate for herself and for others the knowledge and skills she has drawn from that work and to repeat the process in other contexts. Reflection is essential to this distinction.

The goal-setting process described here, which gives shape to the student's aspirations, becomes a key element in reflection. A student who has internalized a concrete set of goals can use them as an ongoing measure of her performance. Reading the environment can also help a student sharpen her sense of her role at her site, giving her another perspective from which to view her activities.

More formal frameworks are introduced into the seminar to give students new ways to think about themselves. One session is devoted to a discussion of Kolb's learning cycle (see Chapter One of this volume). The instructors administer Kolb's learning-style inventory and engage the class in a discussion of different styles and their implications for reflecting on oneself as a learner.

Log keeping, which begins about the fourth week of the OCEL experience, is a major vehicle for teaching students how to reflect. The log used in this seminar is rather open-ended, with directions to choose one or two incidents from the week and reflect on what was learned from them, what questions they raised, what personal insights were achieved, and what challenges were presented. Occasionally, students are asked to reflect on learning styles, or to focus on environmental factors in their internship settings. The students' early logs frequently list tasks or events, often not indicating much about the students' own involvement with them. A student at a counseling site might give a summary of a client's case; a history major working at a county historical society might list all her research tasks. Such listing may well be the first step toward reflection, but by itself it is illuminating for neither reader nor writer. As the semester evolves, however, the level of student reflection increases. Students often refer to issues addressed in the seminar and to their own goals.

Perhaps the most effective way to illustrate this progression is to let the students speak for themselves via extended excerpts from their logs. The first student, Carol, is a prelaw student majoring in social sciences, with minors in global studies and business and management. Her OCEL internship is at a law firm. Her goals for OCEL are the following:

1. Academic: Learn legal jargon, how to do research in the firm's law library.
2. Professional: Begin a networking system that would be very valuable to my legal education and career.
3. Personal: Overcome my shyness around new people, become more outgoing.

Log 1

It was fascinating to watch the legal dance taking place before me— the questions by the attorney and the answers by the plaintiff continued back and forth at a fast pace. I particularly concentrated on the attorney's verbal and nonverbal cues and watched his style of questioning. The plaintiff's answer techniques were interesting as well. This experience was valuable to me because I not only know what a deposition is like from firsthand experience, I am also finding my OCEL experience to reaffirm my career goals. It seems that the more I experience in OCEL, the more I want to learn! I have also learned from my mentor that all depositions are not this interesting, and my next goal is to sit in on a boring deposition and compare the two experiences.

Log 2

Continued my work at the office on the dioxin case. My work is to summarize scientific treatises for the attorneys, and I feel much more comfortable doing this work now as compared to when I first started. I'm sure the reason for that is because I am used to doing them and I am familiar with the formats; however, I also think that I am more comfortable now because I am learning while I am doing the summarizing. If there are scientific words and/or diagnoses that I do not know, I now use an attorney's medical dictionary from the office law library, look up the new term, and write down the definition for future reference. This will help me in the future work that I will do on this case, and my list will also serve as a document of the learning process I went through in OCEL for my own personal use. I like the challenge of new terms, and I also like to learn new words and their meanings. It makes what I am reading more understandable, and this makes me feel that I am doing a good job in OCEL.

Log 3

At the last OCEL seminar, someone had brought up a problem she was having, and both instructors suggested that this student go to the person at the site and ask for a deadline with her project, as well as for some feedback on her work in progress. I acted on this suggestion and over the weekend typed up the notes that I had so far on the civil rights case and took them into work. I asked my mentor if he could look them over and let me know if I was at least on the right track. I think I held my breath while he was reading it over; I was sure he was going to say that I was all wrong. He didn't. In fact, he said that what I had done so far was exactly what he was looking for. He also said that he realized that this case was really hard to do, and that whenever I finished this project was fine with him. Needless to say, I was relieved!

Log 4

Since each case cited in the twenty pages of documents is listed by the names of the litigants, with many letters and numbers after them (reference codes and keys to law books in the library), I really have no idea exactly how the system works, although I am excited and surprised that my supervisor actually gave me something this important to do. I felt excited because I found reading the cases interesting and not as difficult as I had imagined. This gave me some confidence, as I look toward law school and the many cases and briefs ahead of me, that as long as I concentrate and remain positive, I really will be O.K. Also, although I am scared of the prospect of going to the federal library to look up cases, because I'll have no idea where to start, I'm excited by the learning experience that will be! I can attribute this hands-on learning style to my Kolb learning inventory—this is one instance when I would prefer to try to do it myself and learn on my own. And I also have the satisfaction of knowing that through experiences like this, once I am in law school, just think of the "jump" that I will have on my classmates. Research and preparing briefs may not be so foreign to me, compared to someone completely new to the experience, because I will have already done some research through OCEL. My goal is to make very clear which one of my three projects at my site is to be given priority, since time is limited. I will do this by sitting down with my mentor and asking him, as well as talking to the other attorney that I am doing a project for.

Log 5

This experience was also a good lesson for the future. From now on, I will take responsibility and ask where this file will be kept when I am not using it. Part of my frustration was a result of my assuming that any file I need will be on top of my mentor's desk, which I have found to be not quite the case.

Log 6

I also mentioned to my mentor how I've managed to work through some situations in which my shyness started pulling me one way, and I've had to push myself to go another way. I think he was pleased with my work, although he's never come out and said it directly; I've learned that "no news is good news" as far as feedback from him goes, and I can also tell by the turnaround in his attitude/behavior toward me. This change in him, and my own self-assessment of my progress, have made me realize what a success OCEL has been. I have a new sense of confidence in pursuing a career in law.

Anne is an English major with minors in psychology and adult education. Her OCEL site is a public library in a local community. Her goals are:
1. To become familiar with what types of information materials are accessible to the public, and what processing procedures must be used before the information is available for public use.
2. To learn to display a very perceptible self-confidence when tackling an unfamiliar task.
3. To become familiar with the acquisition process for library materials.

Log 1

This week I catalogued sets of classical albums. The process just described is lengthy and monotonous, but it did cause me to think about music and composers, styles and dates of pieces. Although the work itself was tedious, it was a good review of period and styles. I thought that perhaps there might be an easier way of doing paperwork in a library— everything seems so redundant. Perhaps my questioning stems from the fact that I cannot afford to waste time—there is so much to be done and so very little time to do it in.

Log 2

This week's activities, I must admit, were much more varied and interesting, compared to those of last week. First of all, I learned what all those numbers on a catalogue card mean. Until now, I felt very insecure about handling the cards week after week and not knowing everything about them. I asked my mentor to explain every number and group of letters on the card—this she did. I demonstrated to my mentor my earnestness for learning by taking notes as she spoke—I can remember nothing without writing it down.

I feel much better, and along with that feeling, I also am beginning to see the relationship between my tasks and the total library system. Even though I may be doing busy work, I now realize that it is important busy work.

Log 3

Taking Kolb's learning-style inventory reconfirmed my beliefs regarding my learning styles—I like to watch; I like to think—this is how I learn.

This inventory shed light on why my first day at the OCEL site was somewhat uncomfortable. That particular day, I was told to do something. I had no time to think, no time to reflect, no time to feel—I was simply told to do. The task was filing, but I was unfamiliar with the rules. I wanted to sit down with a manual, study, think, pose hypothetical situations to myself, but I could not remember the alphabet, simply because what I was doing was not being done in a way conducive to my learning style.

I am not afraid of tackling any task, but I need the necessary preparation, thought, study, and reflection before attempting anything.

Log 4

I think perhaps my frustration comes from not totally understanding the system in which I am working. I feel ignorant of many aspects of library science, and when I feel that I do not understand something as fully as I can, I become disappointed with myself. This is, of course, a personal struggle, but not feeling in control does lead to self-doubt.

Log 5

This week was exceptionally good because I had more freedom. Instead of working at the same task for several hours, I worked at several tasks for shorter periods. Tuesday I was taught how to check out books—something I had always wanted to do. I practiced several times.

Wednesday I was allowed to do something that I wish I could have done earlier: sit with a cataloguing rulebook and study. My understanding of the system was greatly enhanced by a few hours with this book. It placed the library in its historical context. I became overwhelmed and somewhat irritated at the types and number of rules—it seems impossible to know them all. The amount of exactness, the minute detail—there is so much—but the system contains so much information that preciseness and logic are the only means of ensuring its effective function.

Log 6

I search out important facts and concepts through library journals, publishers' catalogues, and so on. Although I am doing busy work, I am gleaning some special inside knowledge for myself.

I must say that my knowledge of library science was minute when I entered this scene in August, but it has really blossomed into something I can use the rest of my life—that is essentially how I have to regard this OCEL experience, for I know I will probably never work in a library.

Log 7

I had a very good time working with the computer. I learned to put a great deal of information into the computer and have it come out in the form of a beautifully printed set of catalogue cards. I felt very professional doing this type of work; I finally got to use the tools of the trade. My mentor recognizes my need to do diverse things.

Log 8

This week I completed OCEL. I also performed a "stripping" operation. The process is simply placing a metal strip into an obscure spot in a book—it simply causes a magnetic detecting device to sound an alarm. The job was totally mindless, but I did not care, for I had met all the goals I set for myself.

I really am surprised at myself—I took on jobs this week without being asked, and I suggested some new things to my mentor, even catching some mistakes that others had made. After three months, I felt I knew some parts of the system well enough to take some liberties and do tasks that had not been suggested. Judging from my past job experiences, three months is about the time I begin to feel settled in.

The experiences of these two students have served as a means of bringing together their knowing and their doing. The strategies used in the seminar—goal setting, reading the environment, reflecting—have carried over into the way the students have assimilated their work at their sites. Of course, we cannot claim that their learning was entirely the result of the seminar, but neither can we discount the cumulative effect of the strategies used.

While log keeping continues throughout the semester, two assessments are given, at the midpoint and the conclusion of the OCEL experience. These require students to reflect about more abstract dimensions of their work (see Figure 1).

Figure 1. OCEL Assessments

Midsemester Assessment

Imagine that you are your on-site mentor. You have just received a request from the instructors of the OCEL seminar to prepare a midsemester evaluation of your student's performance by describing her working style in detail.

Final Assessment

1. Read through the log forms you have completed this semester.
2. (a) Given that the purpose of log keeping is to facilitate experiential learning, develop a set of criteria for assessing experiential learning.
   (b) Apply the criteria you have generated to the logs you have read. Evaluate the extent to which the learning indicated in them meets the criteria.
3. (a) Describe one behavior pattern that runs through the logs.
   (b) Comment on the learning that this pattern indicates.
   (c) Given this pattern, briefly describe how you might build on it in future learning experiences.

The following assessment excerpts, written by Linda, an English major working at a newspaper office, illustrate the kinds of insights that can be achieved. At midsemester, she writes about her working style:

Linda works in an interesting way. She seems to fluctuate between taking an active role in whatever the work for the day is and being passive—sitting quietly with her mouth shut, although I'm sure she has something to say.

It seems to me that one generalization could be made from this, namely, that when around one or two people who have an action-oriented task to be completed, Linda throws herself into the work wholeheartedly and makes sure that everyone holds up his or her end of the work. For example, when the task is layout or picture printing, Linda steps confidently into the role of leader and takes charge in a very effective way. She moves swiftly when doing these things, but that doesn't prevent her from making a variety of stupid mistakes. She's quick to recognize these mistakes, however, and fixes them shortly after.

If you put her in a bigger group—one that, while task-oriented, isn't physically doing anything—she tends to take notes rather than take charge. She still contributes to the group discussion and participates in decision making, but she just doesn't take the lead.

Linda works best in an active situation, I guess. At least, that's when I see her becoming the most involved and immersed in her work.

Her style is not one of long contemplation followed by action, but instead is action followed by contemplation. After she has jumped into any task, whether it's layout, interviewing, or writing a story, and has completed at least half of it, she stops and thinks about what she should have done to make the project better and more interesting. That's something she should have thought about earlier, even before beginning. Of course, I'm sure she is aware of this slight problem in her work process and, in time, will no doubt change her procedure.

In her final assessment, Linda wrote:

The first issue of the paper left me a bundle of nerves, and I figured all was lost. Now, I just stepped into my pretty comfortable role of leader and set deadlines. I even said, "Don't worry about it," with a kind of nonchalant confidence. I would not have dreamed of doing this three months ago. I suppose it's due to the fact that I now have a little concrete experience under my belt and I know it all works out. I know my commitment to the paper is strong and that I'm responsible enough to make sure all comes out well. I don't have to depend so much on past editors for help (although I'll be forever grateful for their contributions). I can't do it alone, but I can take charge so we do it well.

These two assessments require the students to distance themselves from their experiences. The midsemester assessment, by asking students to assume another's perspective, helps them skirt habitual ways of thinking and often leads to reflective breakthroughs. The final assessment requires another type of distancing: to view experience through self-generated criteria for learning, and to consider the OCEL experience as a whole by drawing generalizations from the complete set of logs. In most cases, students are able to view their experiences with some distance and objectivity and to abstract, from their doing, more sophisticated forms of knowing that can be adapted and applied to future situations.

OCEL experiences such as those described here constitute powerful mechanisms for the integration of knowing and doing, but they are not the first opportunity in the curriculum for students to encounter learning through experience. Because Alverno College has an ability-based curriculum, the students learn through experience beginning with the first semester. This means that they have used some of the strategies of the seminar in various other courses. For example, a number of instructors require students to keep reflective logs to chart their own progress in a course; the syllabus lists course goals and sometimes specifies that students also set learning goals. Many classes use simulations to engage students experientially in the work of the discipline. Often, these are small-group interactions or task-oriented problem-solving discussions about course-related topics and issues. Students do not encounter OCEL as a vastly different experience. True, it is different, but the gap between campus-based learning and off-campus learning is less than it otherwise might be.

One result is that students can move into their OCEL experiences rather quickly, because the time spent to get acclimated is reduced. They bring to their sites some previously developed abilities, which they are then ready to test and further develop. Because they have engaged in reflection about themselves as learners in other contexts, they have a clearer sense of what they want to learn and refine in their abilities.

In the classroom, students are required to apply what they know—to do something with their knowledge. In OCEL, they are asked to know more about what they are doing—to draw meaning from it in relation to their ongoing development as learners. This chapter has provided a closer look at a seminar for off-campus experiential learning, but its guiding strategies and principles are applicable to the goal of bringing knowing and doing together in learning contexts throughout the curriculum.

Allen Wutzdorff is chair of the Experiential Learning Council at Alverno College and a member of the psychology department.

Pat Hutchings is director of the Assessment Forum, a project of the American Association for Higher Education. She is on leave from her position as associate professor of English at Alverno College.

A shared vision of learning characterizes the programs described in this sourcebook.

Conclusion: A View of Learning

Allen Wutzdorff, Pat Hutchings

The seemingly subtle difference between asking what we should teach and asking how students will be different as a result of what we teach can lead to changes that permeate an institution. One of these changes, the one shared by the programs represented in this volume, is a focus on integrating knowledge and experience, on moving beyond the delivery of knowledge to the translation of what students know into what they can do with what they know. Given the context-specific dimensions of such a venture, no single model for such integration has emerged. Nevertheless, the type of learning called for in the programs in this volume is characterized by several shared features.

Each of the approaches begins by defining learning in terms of *outcomes*. That is, the driving question is not one of subject matter only—the *what* of learning—but of results, desired impacts, a vision of how the student will be different. Course materials and methods are directed toward producing specified changes in students, changes not only in what they know but in what they can do.

Moreover, these outcomes are specified not only for individual courses but across courses, and in some cases across the curriculum. Admittedly, beginning students may see their learning in distinct units—in a course-by-course fashion—but each of the programs described here is designed

P. Hutchings and A. Wutzdorff (eds.). *Knowing and Doing: Learning Through Experience.*
New Directions for Teaching and Learning, no. 35. San Francisco: Jossey-Bass, Fall 1988.

to promote the integration process. Students are encouraged to draw relationships between what they learn in, say, psychology with philosophy courses; they are increasingly expected to connect classroom learning to life experiences as well. The learning described in this volume is defined in terms of larger, longer-term expectations and outcomes, with the aim of developing in students concepts and abilities that can be carried into new situations. *Transferability* of learning is a key feature.

A related characteristic is a focus on *performance*. To think of learning as performance is to think in terms of acting out, or applying what is learned. Performance is the *integration* of knowing and doing, a kind of learning in which the student is actively engaged and involved, whether it be in performing a piano concerto, solving an engineering design problem, or writing a report on marketing strategies for a local firm.

At the same time, the programs in this volume require that students step back from involvement in order to reflect on their learning and themselves as learners. Underlying each approach is the distinction between experience for its own sake and experience that leads to learning through a process of *reflection*. Students are asked to think seriously about themselves as learners, to learn how they learn and how they can learn more powerfully. They are asked to write about themselves as learners, examine their learning styles, and assess their performance. Faculty-defined outcomes provide a yardstick for such reflection, but eventually students generate their own definitions of successful performance and become self-directed learners.

The learning described and called for in this volume, then, can be characterized by its focus on broadly defined, performance-based outcomes, by its combination of active involvement and self-reflection, and by an increasing integration of knowing and doing. Under what conditions can such learning be engendered? What institutional or program-wide implications follow?

First, perhaps, comes a high degree of institutional self-consciousness. Each of the chapters in this volume speaks of a shared vision of purposes, a set of collectively derived objectives. Faculty are seen as specialists in their fields but also as professional educators in a broader sense, working with individuals in other disciplines to articulate and achieve larger outcomes; they are called upon to rethink their disciplines in terms of overall patterns of student learning and how various courses contribute to outcomes that equip students for life beyond the classroom. In this sense, the programs in this volume come from a willingness to ask hard questions about the nature and purpose of education. Rather than accepting as givens the conventional methods of "taking" courses and "covering" material (the metaphors are suggestive), they look toward what will, in the long run, stand students in good stead.

Second, each of these programs is not only clear about purposes but committed to achieving them. College catalogues typically offer assurances that graduates will be prepared to participate in society as contributing citizens, make informed decisions, and become future leaders, and so on, yet on many campuses these outcomes are not explicitly taught. What is clear in examining the programs set forth in this volume is that such purposes are not left to chance. Desired outcomes are not assumed but planned for; the integration and translation of what students know into what they can do is systematically built into teaching methods and the curriculum.

Pat Hutchings and Allen Wutzdorff team-taught an interdisciplinary seminar at Alverno College for all students participating in a required Off-Campus Experiential Learning program. Both have chaired Alverno's campuswide committee on experiential learning.

Index

Please remember that this is a library book,
and that it belongs only temporarily to each
person who uses it. Be considerate. Do
not write in this, or any, library book.

Table of Contents

Introduction

Dear Puzzler,

When I see the word *America*, I don't just see a word. What I see is an enormous and beautiful pageantry of places, people, and their creations—the mighty roar of Niagara Falls, the acrobatic pirouettes of a skater in New York City, and the golden rays of the rising sun glinting off The Gateway Arch of St. Louis.

What I love most about America is that the brilliant diversity of her landscapes and cities is equally matched by the brilliant diversity of her people!

These puzzles invite you to take in all the sights and challenge you to spot the differences. Each puzzle features at least five things that have been changed in pictures that may seem identical at first glance. Now turn the page and go have some cross-country fun!

Sincerely,
Rick Schwab

KEEN

Start your journey across America with these puzzles that will help you keen your ability to spot five differences while you sightsee across the states.

110830 **Answer on page 126**

A Native American gathering in Milwaukee, Wisconsin

Answer on page 126

Answer on page 127

Preparing for Launch at Cape Canaveral, Florida

Answer on page 127

Answer on page 128

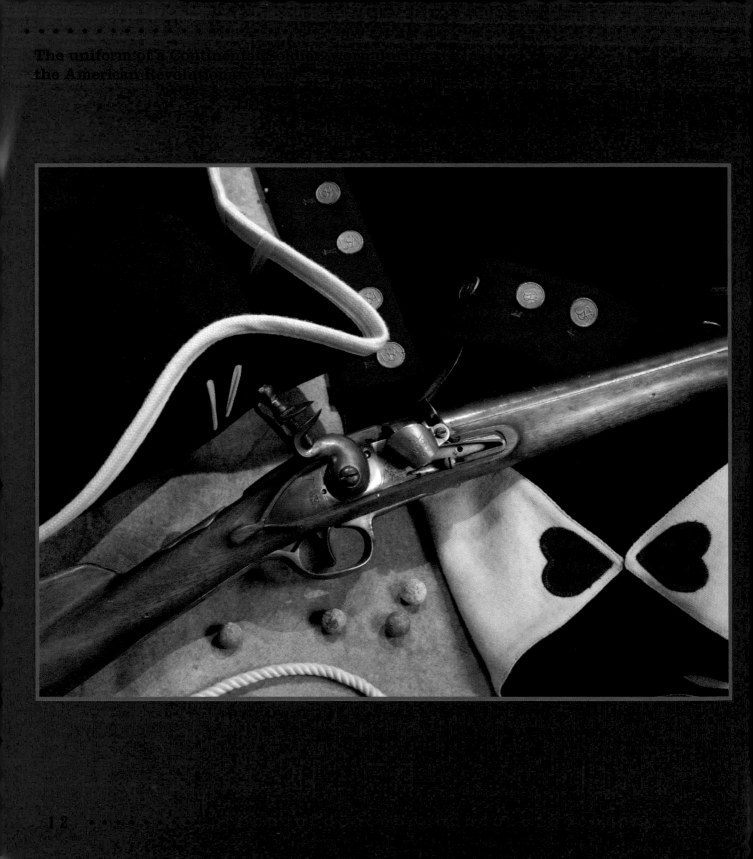

Answer on page 128

Answer on page 129

A sunset over the Gulf of Mexico seen from Florida's west coast

Answer on page 129

16

A hat stand for winter tourists in New York City, New York

Answer on page 130

Answer on page 131

A patriotic pooch

Answer on page 132

Elegance in a traditional American quilt

Answer on page 132

Answer on page 183

A classic "Woodie" station wagon

Answer on page 134

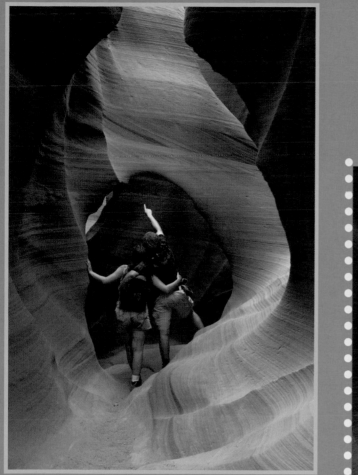

Answer on page 134

Touchdown!

Answer on page 135

Answer on page 135

Answer on page 136

Answer on page 136

Answer on page 137

Answer on page 137

The dogwood tree is native to North America.

Answer on page 138

Answer on page 138

Answer on page 139

Answer on page 139

Elvis Presley's modest birthplace in Tupelo, Mississippi

Answer on page 140

The Montauk Lighthouse on eastern Long Island, New York

Answer on page 140

There's always a rainbow in the mist of Niagara Falls.

Answer on page 141

Answer on page 141

A car show in a small New Jersey town

Answer on page 142

A tornado in Colorado

Houses
For Sale
super-cheap!
going fast!
006-516-3241

Answer on page 142

SHARP

Take a good look at these sights! These classic American scenes maybe familiar, but you'll need to look sharp to see six things you've been missing.

Answer on page 143

A replica of the Declaration of Independence

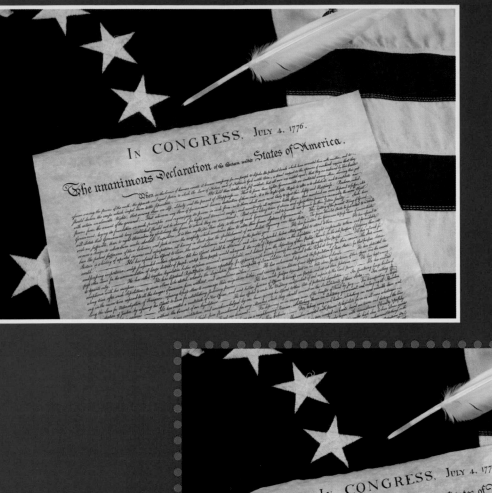

Answer on page 143

Answer on page 144

The Capitol Rotunda in Washington, D.C.

Answer on page 144

Answer on page 145

A barn on the Nathan Hale Homestead in Connecticut

Answer on page 145

A replica of a paddle wheel riverboat on the Savannah River in Georgia

Answer on page 146

A view of lower Manhattan over the Brooklyn Bridge

Answer on page 146

An Irish American parade commemorating The Battle of Brooklyn—the largest battle in the American Revolutionary War

Answer on page 147

Answer on page 147

The Grover balloon in New York City's Thanksgiving Day Parade

Answer on page 148

Answer on page 148

Answer on page 149

Answer on page 149

A shopping mall in White Plains, New York

Answer on page 150

Answer on page 150

Answer on page 151

Answer on page 151

Answer on page 152

Answer on page 152

Answer on page 153

Answer on page 153

An art deco building in Miami, Florida

Answer on page 154

A countryside scene outside Woodbridge, Virginia

Answer on page 155

Answer on page 155

A Kiss tribute concert in Charlotte, North Carolina

Answer on page 156

An historic plantation home in southern Louisiana

Answer on page 156

Answer on page 157

A great sequoia in Yosemite National Park, California

Answer on page 157

Answer on page 158

Answer on page 158

Answer on page 159

MASTERFUL

●　●　●　●　●　○　○　○　○　○　○　○

These American beauties are an eyeful! They will take a masterful observer to spot the seven differences. Look hard and you'll discover things you have never seen before in this great land.

Answer on page 159

Answer on page 160

The Walt Disney Concert Hall by architect
Frank Gehry in Los Angeles, California

Answer on page 160

Answer on page 161

Participants in the annual Coney Island Mermaid
Parade in Brooklyn, New York

Answer on page 161

Answer on page 162

Mystic Seaport, Connecticut

Answer on page 162

Answer on page 163

Answer on page 163

Answer on page 164

Two buffaloes take a shortcut in Yellowstone
National Park, Wyoming.

Answer on page 164

A Texas pump jack

Answer on page 165

Answer on page 165

Answer on page 166

One of the first American cars

Answer on page 166

Answer on page 167

Answer on page 167

Old Faithful, a geyser in Yellowstone National Park, Wyoming

Answer on page 168

Answer on page 168

Answer on page 169

The "400 at the Brickyard" race at the Indianapolis Speedway in Indiana

Answer on page 169

Answer on page 170

Answer on page 170

A rollercoaster outside of Los Angeles, California

Answer on page 171

Answer on page 171

Answer on page 172

A typical small farm

Answer on page 172

Answer on page 173

A traditional Hawaiian luau

Answer on page 173

Answer on page 174

Union Station in Los Angeles, California

Answer on page 174

Answer on page 175

Putting the pieces of America together

Answer on page 175

ANSWERS

Puzzle pages 6-7

Puzzle page 8

Puzzle page 9

Puzzle page 10

Puzzle page 11

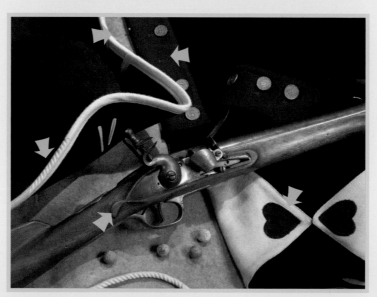

Puzzle pages 12-13

Puzzle pages 14-15

Puzzle page 16

Puzzle page 17

Puzzle page 18

Puzzle page 19

Puzzle page 20

Puzzle page 21

Puzzle page 22

Puzzle page 23

Puzzle pages 24-25

Puzzle page 26

Puzzle page 27

Puzzle page 28

Puzzle page 29

Puzzle page 30

Puzzle page 31

Puzzle page 32

Puzzle page 33

Puzzle page 34

Puzzle page 35

Puzzle page 36

Puzzle page 37

Puzzle page 38

Puzzle page 39

Puzzle page 40

Puzzle page 41

Puzzle pages 42-43

Houses
For Sale
super-cheap!
going fast!
006-516-1141

Puzzle page 44

Puzzle pages 46-47

Puzzle page 48

Puzzle page 49

Puzzle page 50

Puzzle page 51

Puzzle page 52

Puzzle page 53

Puzzle pages 54-55

Puzzle page 56

Puzzle page 57

Puzzle page 58

Puzzle page 59

Puzzle page 60

Puzzle page 61

Puzzle page 62

Puzzle page 63

Puzzle pages 64-65

Puzzle page 66

Puzzle page 67

Puzzle page 68

Puzzle page 69

Puzzle pages 70-71

Puzzle page 72

Puzzle page 73

Puzzle page 74

Puzzle page 75

Puzzle page 76

Puzzle page 77

Puzzle pages 78-79

Puzzle page 80

Puzzle page 81

Puzzle pages 82-83

Puzzle page 84

Puzzle pages 86-87

Puzzle page 88

Puzzle page 89

Puzzle pages 90-91

Puzzle page 92

Puzzle page 93

Puzzle page 94

Puzzle page 95

Puzzle page 96

Puzzle page 97

Puzzle pages 98-99

Puzzle page 100

Puzzle page 101

Puzzle pages 102-103

Puzzle page 104

Puzzle page 105

Puzzle pages 106-107

Puzzle page 108

Puzzle page 109

Puzzle page 110

Puzzle page 111

Puzzle page 112

Puzzle page 113

Puzzle pages 114-115

Puzzle page 116

Puzzle page 117

Puzzle page 118

Puzzle page 119

Puzzle page 120

Puzzle page 121

Puzzle page 122

Puzzle page 123

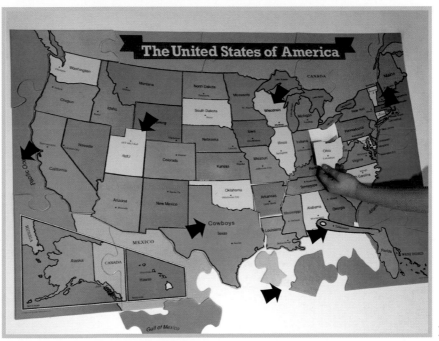

Puzzle page 124

CREDITS

The images appearing on the following pages are © by Rick Schwab:
12-13, 14-15, 16, 18, ... 55, 56, 75, 78-79, 80, 86, 87, 88, 90, 91, 92, 93, ...

The uniform and mu... ...urtesy of The Old Stone House Museum in Bro...

The images appearing ... el Alicia:
50, 69, 89, 122

The image on page 17...

The images appearing ... photo.com:
20, 21, 23, 38, 46-47, ...

The remainder of the ... Shutterstock.com.